Water Gardening
Indoors and Out

Water Gardening Indoors and Out

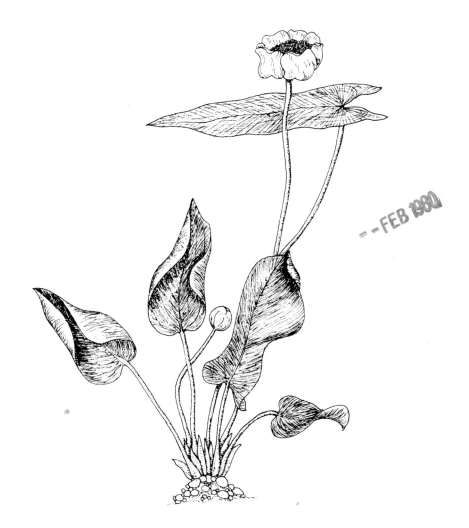

Reginald Dutta

Drawings by Rosanne McConachie

B. T. Batsford Ltd, London

Other books by Reginald Dutta include:
Tropical Fish
Beginner's Guide to Tropical Fish and Fish Tanks
Manual for Fish Tank Owners
Right Way to Keep Pet Fish
Encyclopedia of Tropical Fish
Tropical Fish and Fish Tanks

and, under the name his friends call him, Rex Dutta:
Reality of Occult/Yoga/Meditation/Flying Saucers
Flying Saucer Message
Flying Saucer Viewpoint

First published in Great Britain 1977 by
B. T. Batsford Ltd,
4 Fitzhardinge Street, London W1H 0AH

Designed and produced by Walter Parrish
International Limited, London

Printed and bound in Great Britain by Purnell & Sons Ltd

ISBN 0 7134 0886 3

To the plants, the fish, the customers,
and the staff of Fish Tanks Limited,
49 Blandford St, London W1,
without whose mutual help and co-operation
this knowledge might never have been gained.

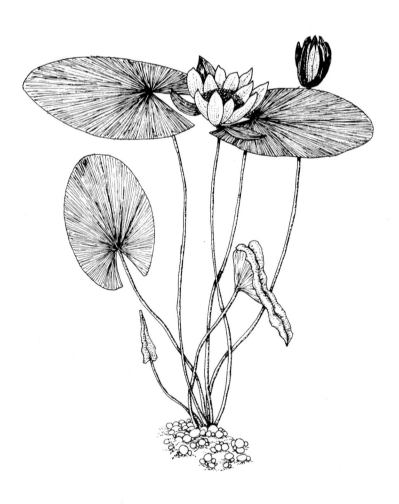

contents

introduction

The aim of this book is to focus on the plants: their wonderful variety, the uplift that they can give you in a gentle, yet very pervading way; asking so little from you in care or attention, content to be left unattended for long periods while you are absent; yet ever ready to welcome you back, to show you their new growths, to sway in response to your smile; they will soothe your cares, ease your hurry, your rush, your tension.

They will give you a quietly sustaining strength of green harmony that perhaps you do not fully expect.

So many lovely factors help to maintain the balance of the tank containing underwater plants, a balance that lasts and lasts and lasts, hardly needing to be touched:

soil, plain or coloured, earthy or gay;

aquascaping as rocks combine with soil to make beautiful terraces, hills, hollows, rings, cliffs—fascinating, be they traditional or adventurous, as you can see from the photographs;

ornaments added to lights and streaming air bubbles, dancing in soft therapeutic sounds and causing the plant leaves to bend, and murmur in the gently flowing waters.

Whether you add fish or not, lavish colour or not, have a big tank or not, you will have happiness. You will have light, movement and pleasure. You will have a wholeness, subtly permeating.

And you will have very few calls on your time, or purse.

A brief look at the organization of the book: to deal first with some general principles of growing plants in water and then to discuss the creation of an indoor growing environment, with basic guidance on choosing equipment, locations and so on.

These factors are universal, wherever you live, and on the whole they do not change with every passing fashion. Plants are concentrated on throughout rather than fish—of course both are an essential part of any display in an aquarium, but plants are here considered in their own right. That is the aim of the book.

The central part of the book is two sequences of pages running in parallel. In one sequence are shown a series of plant arrangements, each one pictured and described on a separate double-page opening, to bring home to you the wonderful possibilities offered by an imaginative plant set-up. The other sequence gives drawings of plants grouped very broadly according to their visual effect, their own special role, in a display. For most lovers of underwater plants the way they look is the important thing and the most practical way of classifying them, rather than according to botanical genera and species.

After indoor displays the book moves on to a similar treatment of plants grown in outdoor ponds and watery surroundings.

Finally, we look at hydroponics, the art of growing house-plants in water without soil. Ideal for the modern apartment-dweller, convenient for everyone.

When referring to a particular species, we have generally used the botanical, scientific name, as this is more precise and is understood internationally. Common names often change from country to country. At the end of the book will be found an Index giving scientific names and many common names of the plants mentioned. We have aimed at showing as wide a selection of plants as possible, and this is why the range of plant line-drawings extends, rather than coincides exactly with, the plants pictured in the tank arrangements. Certain plants, such as Lilies, are available in such a wide range that we have left their detailed coverage to the conventional gardening books; we have deliberately concentrated, in our detailed drawings, on the more unusual plants.

Here, then, is a pastime which is creative, and which offers a contact with the natural world of plants in an unusual area, a hobby which requires little space and relatively little financial outlay, and which will enhance any room or garden.

creating an eco-system indoors

water

Everything your plants need to flourish has to be there—in the water. You will be housing plant growths from far-away tropical lands of moist heat, arid sun, swampy lakes, monsoons, rivulets, fast-flow and forests; all, but all must be catered for by the water in your tank.

Wonder of wonders, this is easy to achieve; mankind merely has to follow Mother Nature's golden rules, have just a dash of intuitive intelligence, a harmonious working with the plants, an understanding of their feelings and needs, and everything will be just fine.

Let's start with the top of the water, which should be clean, free of dust and of oily scum, so that fresh oxygen can be absorbed, and harmful gases like carbon dioxide expelled. Dragging a sheet of newspaper across the surface, rather like a housewife skimming the fat off soup, will enhance this process; so will aeration, or preferably aeration combined with a filter; and so will live, floating plants, which do help to keep the surface moving.

The water itself will soon become 'mature' even if taken straight from the tap; that is to say that minute micro-organisms will be born therein, and these teeming but unseen life-forms are a beneficial source of food and of nourishment. Although hostile bacteria can also be produced, this would happen only if the 'balance' of the tank had been upset, eg by an excess of dirt, mulm, green algae, or other such carelessness of an obvious kind.

Normally, the 'balance' will last for a long, long time, and with a minimum of attention, such as a periodic half-change of tank water, especially if the air surface is less than 24″×12″ for depths of 24-30".

Real enthusiasts will concern themselves with the hardness of water (the DH, or parts per million of solids) and the acid/alkaline condition (the pH), and will be buying themselves all sorts of fascinating gadgets to measure, correct and change them. Let us start with the American measurement of one degree of hardness—1.0, the German equivalent is 1.8, and the British is 0.7, so please be careful when reading foreign papers on how 'soft' the water is! We have used the British units in this book, but conversion, if necessary, is quite simple. Hardness can also be measured in parts per million.

However, all nations have agreed that 7.0 is the neuter point of the acid/alkaline range or pH, which for plant purposes goes from 5.5 to 8.5, with an optimum for practical use of pH 6.6-7.2. Tank readings vary from night to morning as plants switch from making oxygen during daylight to releasing carbon deposits plus carbon dioxide gas at night.

A tell-tale sign of pH imbalance would be white precipitate particles forming on the leaves in the morning, and then dissolving during the day. A change of tank water will help.

Most people will just not need to bother with these technicalities. The plants will soon begin to nag you if things are not right: they will refuse to grow, will droop, will shed leaves, will change their very shape/colour/texture, will develop blemishes, spots and marks, till finally you catch on and frantically consult our section 'Things that go wrong' (page 18).

Then, the balance restored, the plants will soon forgive you, and sheen their greenery as only they can do.

Balancing the tank means a sensible allocation of priorities: of sand/soil rich enough to sustain but not to cloud the water; aeration strong enough to break surface, to sweep the whole tank without leaving festering backwaters; filters big enough actually to remove dirt and not to get clogged up too quickly; the right temperature—just a heater/thermostat will do; and lighting adequate for the job, but not so excessive as to be harsh. Add rocks, as described later, and beauty and easy balance will give you trouble-free joy.

Let's take it step by step.

soil/sand
Easy does it; shovelling in loam, fertilizers, and the rest can very, very soon be overdone. In fact, you could need none at all: the natural and slow accumulation of dust/debris, or the droppings of a few fish (should you decide to have them as a

background adjunct) or the occasional injection of plant-fertilizer liquids (or solids; they come in both forms) would be ample.

Perhaps the biggest cause of hostile bacteria, and hence of trouble, is over-rich planting medium. A depth of 2″ is adequate, but greater depths can be a further safeguard as well as being decorative when aquascaped, as is obvious from the photographs scattered throughout this book.

If the sand/planting-medium is too fine it 'mats down' and tends to choke the roots as well as clogging the filters; if it is too coarse, the delicate 'hair roots' have difficulty working round the particles and thus expansion gets inhibited.

Artificially made substitutes now abound, ground to $\frac{1}{16}$″ (ie the grains would go through a sieve with holes of that diameter), and in lovely shades of colours—as shown in our colour plates. Incidentally, other sizes may certainly be used, $\frac{1}{8}$″ or $\frac{3}{16}$″ as we illustrate, but anything larger than that does slow down root-growth. Beware of too-cheap substitutes, where the dye is not fast and the material used is toxic. 'Inert' is the technical term for what we need. This means that there is no reaction with the water; no effect on the pH (acid/alkaline balance) or the DH (hardness), for instance.

With the growth of hydroponics has come a stream of artificial planting aids, granular-based, clay-based, peat-based—usually sold under brand-names and usually providing stimulus to growth.

lighting
Please don't just dump a bulb on top, and then stand back smirking in hope. In Nature the light varies in intensity, and in position; mankind can easily reproduce that with a combination of top lights plus auxiliary sidelights; even a time-switch could be incorporated to ring the changes regularly.

All manner of lovely lights are widely available: daylight types, pin-pointed beams, diffused all-over spreads; speciality types to emphasize particular colours of the spectrum; infra-red; and many more.

If your tank is getting smothered with green algae, then you've obviously made the lights too strong, or you've forgotten that even one hour of sunlight represents millions of candlepower. Equally, please don't go to the other extreme, dismal gloom, so that your plants take on a jaundiced, yellow-wilt expression.

About ten hours' artificial light per day in a normally bright room (but free of direct sun on the tank) at a strength of 30 watts per square foot, held approximately 4″ above water level, is standard procedure.

Plants tend to 'rest' in winter, and are accustomed to the lessened light that Mother Nature arranges for the quiet period. Of course, Man has invented the jet aircraft and hurtles plants from 'summer' to 'winter' in one day, and then complains that plants wilt; but all is usually well after a little leaf-shedding.

heat
Naturally plants prefer your tank to have temperatures similar to those they were born into, but they adapt quite rapidly to suit your whim. Almost anything from 68° to 78°F (20–25°C) will do

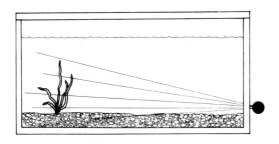

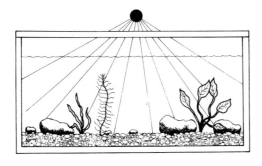

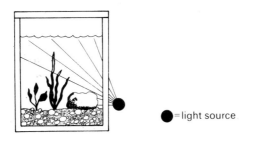

● =light source

Three basic ways to light your fish tank. Top to bottom: Using a narrow beam to highlight a particular plant or feature; general, diffuse, overhead lighting; diffuse lighting from *behind,* to bathe plants and rocks in an ethereal and mysterious glow.

13

for the vast majority of tropical plants.

Of course, plants can pout and can sulk and can nag: have you ever had to stand up to the lovely, green, delicately tall, symmetrically whorled Cabomba plant when it decides to go 'slimy' because the tank is too hot (above 80°F or 26°C) and you've been too slow to do something about it? It's enough to make strong men melt.

Incidentally, cooling a tank can be quite a problem. Ice cubes hung in a sealed plastic bag (clean! no smell!) can be helpful; once melted their water should be removed and not be allowed to mingle with the tank, unless you know that the newly-melted water is fit to drink and hence to go into your tank. Or you can coil (clean!) hosepipe tubing in your tank and run cold water through.

Heating the tank is not difficult now that heaters and thermostats are available in pet shops, specialist dealers and supermarkets. Just make sure that the all-over distribution of heat is reasonably uniform.

Under-gravel heaters, below-tank-base heaters and the like are positively harmful, as plants always keep their *roots* cool in Mother Nature, and have heat only higher up. If your tank is sited above a radiator then your plants will gang-up on you by wilting, and make you move it, or at least insulate the base.

aeration and filtration
This is possibly one of the most helpful of aids to easy growth and clear, sweet, clean tanks. Tremendous technical progress has been made in the past two decades and you have a very fine choice indeed of pumps and filters. Skimping on this vital equipment could be poor judgement.

Under-gravel filters are available with ridged bases, slotted bases, cave-like bases; with more than one outlet, with fast-flow outlets, with outlets passing through extra filtration units, or vitamin stimulant units, or units to make the water soft/acid/ peaty/ionized/sterilized; to cover the whole base of the tank; to snake through chosen areas; to slope so that the covering sand can be deeper at one end; to be free of outlet-tubes and air-lifts, and to release the air below gravel; to have reverse-flow so that the dirt is pushed from under the gravel out into the water to be caught there by auxiliary filters.

Immersion filters can be housed inside the tank to trap the dirt—round ones, triangular ones to slot into the corners, vertical ones, horizontal ones, L-shaped ones, with re-usable cartridges of filter materials, disposable cartridges, multiple cartridges. Immersion filters float on tank water, or are housed in the tank-top light cover.

Incredible is the range.

Outside filters that have single chambers, or multiple chambers each housing a different filter medium (coarse, fine, or activated); water that is lifted with air-assistance to give extreme flow; a fully-swirled-to-saturation mix of air in the tank water; heated air lifts to warm the water; sterilizing air lifts to kill bacteria.

What a choice!

And, there is a new generation of pumps to give the increased power now demanded. They are far more silent and reliable and include all manner of refinements like slide-controls to phase down the power (not merely to clamp tight the air-line flow to throttle it down while the pump rattles on at full rate) but actually to reduce the electrical power production at source, to give extra silence for night use. Pumps can flow 20 gallons per hour or even 500 gallons per hour.

All these are available at a reasonableness of price that is a tribute to the march of technology. Even the magnetic-drive power-filters that will run continuously for month after month cost little more than a meal out for two.

The filter area must be big enough not to clog up for at least seven days, otherwise you pour poisoned water back from a stinking filter, and do great harm.

The rate of flow should be sufficient to re-cycle the whole tank at least once a day, if not once an hour.

The strength of the return flow of filtered water should sweep all areas of the tank and not leave swampy back-waters; additional air outlets can be positioned to ensure this.

The air outlets can be served by the many different air stones; more porous for finer bubbles, more coloured for greater swirl; more elongated for curtain-effect, as the bubbles rise, along a run of 12″ or more, in a continuous vertical stream.

What more could your plants or you ask?

Please don't skimp on this equipment.

rocks and plants

Rocks are essential to beauty—protective to plants, to small crustaceans like snails; to alternate shade with light; to block, bounce or divert the flow of water returning from a filter; and, above all, vital to hold, maintain and stabilize the aquascape you create.

Aquatic rocks should be hard, very slow indeed to dissolve in water; otherwise the balance of your tank will constantly be upset. Those easily-weathered soft stones, often full of holes and hollows, should be avoided. Your specialist dealer will advise you; a rough guide is to scrape the rock surface with a penknife (it should not powder or allow deep etchings on its surface); or to drop household-strength hydrochloric acid onto it to see if interaction with the rock takes place, especially with quartz-veined rocks. Your exact choice of rocks will depend on availability where you live—just follow these general principles.

The range of rocks that can be used is tremendous. Coloured rocks, artificial or coral; plastic imitation rocks that are light in weight and are already moulded or locked into sizeable formations; all these have a role to play. You can use glazed tiles, or glazed strips like artificial walls; glass, ceramic, or porcelain; plastic cut into loops, curves, bubbles, hollow balls, or spider's-web threads.

All these materials, provided they are 'inert', are there for your ingenuity to combine colour with shape with tradition with modernity.

Worthy of your home, your plants grow snug and proud and tall in their hollows, in their terraces, in their arrow-formations, star patterns, circular rings; in their shady glades, their half-hidden cave entrances, their open-space clearings; with single chosen plants expanding in height and scope, with leafy

16

clumps, with shy little bushes, with towering upward growth.

Profusely reproduced throughout these pages is a representative sample of the vast range of plants that Mother Nature provides for your use. Botanical technicalities are perhaps inappropriate for most of us, and broad groupings such as 'floating plants', 'submersive' (those that stay below water level and trail along the top), and 'emersive' (the ones that break surface to emerge and to flower above) are probably more helpful. This is broadly the approach we have adopted in grouping the plant drawings, which taken together with the photographs show a fantastic range. Most of the plants illustrated should be available either naturally or through dealers wherever you live—but if you can't find the exact species you want for a display then just use one related to it which looks similar. The effect will be just as beautiful.

In actual life, the plants have been taught adaptability by drought, wind, and flood, and should easily cope with your tank conditions.

Grown from shoots, or runners, a plant will come with roots already developed. It should be fleshy round the root-stock so that it carries its own emergency supply of sustenance to feed it through the strain of transplanting; even if all the leaves are shed, it will still grow afresh if the root-stock is healthy. Plants should have the roots well spread/embedded but the 'crown' should not be buried beyond the point where the white of the roots gives way to the green of the stem.

Many of the submersive or trailing types are propagated from cuttings, and will soon develop their own roots. When tall they often shed their lower leaves, and the stalky effect can be accentuated by adverse conditions; first, find out why the plant is unhappy, next nip off the lower stalky part and re-plant the bushy top as if it were a new cutting. Arranged in groups, clusters and thickets they are more pleasing than as isolated single stems.

As a rough rule of thumb the lighter the green colour the more the plant absorbs as sustenance from its foliage, and the more it is susceptible to reduced light; but it will take overcrowding fairly easily and will be content in clumps.

The heavy-rooted emersent plants can grow almost in any light, any soil, any temperature; they are so tough (fish don't like eating their bitter-tasting leaves, but love to peck at the micro-organisms living on their broad surfaces) because of the harsh treatment that Mother Nature metes out when the summer sun dries up the water to expose much of the foliage to

'G—B

heat and to swarming insects, and then to a monsoon flood which rises to several feet of water depth, so that the plant is engulfed in débris and mulm carried by the rushing waters.

No wonder these plants will flourish in your tank, and soon expand to fill all the space you allocate. Again that good old rule of thumb—the more you nip off the emerging shoots the more the plant will grow laterally/bush-like. Pruning off the outer leaves, like the tough outer leaves of a cabbage, encourages fresh growth.

Some of us would be shattered to be told to talk to our plants. 'Green fingers' are merely the subtle but real emanations below the level of the dense physical, down in the flowing-softness of the psychic level, and talking to the plants causes immediate response; believe it or not, plants have feelings that range further than mere frost/sun, and really will 'sense you' if you make friends with them, allow the power of your thought to encourage and help them. Everyone realises that planting is best done in season; gentler, more responsive owners are aware that many other delicate factors help growth—such as planting during the rising moon, rather than the waning half of the month. It's not only tides (water) that the moon affects! The green harmony, the gently pervading strength, the very basics of Mother Nature, that healthy plants can flow back to mankind is the inner reason we all like (and *need*) them.

things that go wrong
If your plants begin to change colour/shape/texture then they are reacting to the balance operative in your tank.

When first transplanted from the totally different conditions of their native habitat, perhaps in another continent, of course they will wilt. The sensible purchase is not, therefore, of the biggest specimen available, but of the healthiest, the freshest, the youngest.

A pellet of clay, or of the widely sold artificial planting media, inserted at the base of the site on transplanting is helpful. If, however, you are resiting many specimens, then the addition of liquid fertilizer might be better.

If dark patches develop in the base sand round the plant roots, then hostile bacteria are over-abundant: too much fertilizer, too many plants for the area available, insufficient filtration, too much/too little light or heat, oily scum on the water surface, base sand not deep enough (less than 1″ for a plant 4″ high)—these are obvious problems that can be checked at a glance.

If the plant develops blemishes, spots, and distorted foliage (over-curled leaves, knotted stalks, etc) then the affected parts should be sharply pruned.

The pH and DH may also need to be checked if the imbalance has gone too far. A gadget for testing the level of hostile nitrites can also be used.

Fluoride in the tap water is in my view harmful, no matter what the 'interested parties' say to the contrary. It is a nerve gas used to tame wild animals, or to keep inmates docile in a prison or in a concentration camp; and its inhibiting effect on plant life is marked. Boiling does not remove it from tap water; rainwater or distilled water could be used to lessen the retarding effect on plants, and increased filtration could be tried.

Plants from humid, moist Asia have never met a cold draught of air before coming to you, and shrivel in horror; you'll need to be extra careful when lifting off the tank cover in a very cold room. It would perhaps be useful to drop the water-level an inch or so to allow more protective glass to surround the air at the surface otherwise too brutally exposed to cold draughts.

Finally, the good old rule: when in doubt part-change the water and/or the planting medium.

building a set-up

A good set-up should hold its form for a long time; if it is poorly done then the sand will soon slop all over the place and obliterate the design. The whole secret is in the firmness with which the rocks are anchored deep into the sand, in their shape, and in their size which is far bigger out of water than appears to be the case when they are sited in the tank. You would perhaps be surprised to learn that we put a hundredweight of aquarium rocks into a $24'' \times 12'' \times 15''$ tank when doing a full aquascape. Just plonking a few in a semi-circle and jabbing in a handful of plants is unlikely to produce the beautiful effect we are aiming for.

Our three photographs illustrate the process. The tank is only $18'' \times 10'' \times 10''$ and the first shock is to realise that 28 lb of thoroughly washed sand is required, piled up, to hold the design. The next shock is to find that the first photograph holds such 'enormous' rocks: left-hand flange $5'' \times 3''$; right-hand flange $5'' \times 4''$; rear column $3\frac{1}{2}'' \times 2\frac{1}{2}''$; triple steps, each $3'' \times 2''$. Look how deeply the two flanges are embedded, firmly to grip the shape, and to maintain the rising pile; by way of comparison the heater tube on the right is $6'' \times 1''$.

Notice too how there are no gaps left to allow the sand to dribble out later: the two flanges and the top two steps are tightly united; the rear column's embedded base holds the rear jammed against the tank glass. If the tank were larger and the sand pile were higher, then the bottom step would have to be long enough to make direct contact underneath the sand with the two flanges; ie it would be some $6''$ long, virtually as big as the right-hand flange itself, although only a tiny part would show above the sand.

Now it is easy to understand why the $3''$ bare foreground of

Opposite, top and bottom: The first and second stages in building an aquascape.

the tank will remain so, unswamped by drifting sand, and why the plants will be able to root and thrive when planted.

The second photograph on page 21 shows the anchoring of a gentle slope. Notice again how the three centre rocks are in tight contact, as are the two extreme flanges with the glass. No gaps are left for sand to dribble through. It is important to realise just how much is buried. The full rock sizes, from left to right, are: front row, Somerset 4″×2″ (hiding the glass heater), Devon (flat/squat) 3″×2½″, right-hand quartz 3″×3″; back row, all three 3″×3″ even though the right-hand flange looks much smaller because it is buried that much deeper to hold back the sand. These particular rocks have been used because they are beautiful and easily available. Wherever you live, you can use the rocks available to you in your own locality, following the general guidelines given on page 16.

The photograph below shows the use of a 7″×3″ Devon rock to complete the arch. In this photograph too we see plants in position for the first time. They have plenty of sand depth for their roots, and fall naturally into groups. Notice how delicate plants are used to soften the hard lines of the rock faces, and partially to obscure cave entrances or crevices. Please notice too how the rocks themselves harmonize with flat slate, vertical veining, and squat gleaming quartz; how the most attractive faces of the rock have been hand-chipped to shape to bring out their inherent 'character' all the more. (We hold the rocks in a soft cloth, and tap patiently 'along the grain' when shaping them.)

Notice especially that none, but none, of the functional heaters/thermostats/thermometers/filters are allowed to show. Beauty prevails, unobscured.

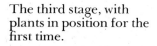

The third stage, with plants in position for the first time.

some simple
plant-groups

Beautiful effects can be achieved with quite simple resources.
Here are illustrated some simple plant arrangements, to show
you some of the principles of contrast and balance.

In the upper photograph on page 24, the plants are arched
in a pleasing contrasting setting of Devon rock and Channel
Island sea-sand.

The stout Sagittaria grass-like clump in the left foreground
has been trimmed to balance the not-too-common Acorus
groups on the right; these latter tend to stay short, stumpy and
bushy and are admirable for 'screening' the rock crevice and
slab.

The big Bacopa to the rear left arches with the paler green of
the Wisteria to the rear right, and will maintain this posture if
the overhead top light is centred at the arch top.

In the second photograph the arrangement is reversed by
grouping the rocks heavily in the centre, and then surrounding
them, forest-like, with loose-flowing, slightly untidy plants
which would sway gently if air bubbles were played into the
tank.

The particular plants shown in this arrangement do not need
heated water, and can survive in poor light if you want to
dispense with the tank cover. From left to right they are: the
well-known Hornwort, found everywhere; the Money Plant,
also widely spread over the continents; Myriophyllum, again
easily available. Just for photographic contrast we have put a
clump of tropical Myriophyllum on the extreme right, so that
you can the more clearly distinguish them.

The third arrangement on page 24 shows rather more prized
plants, and, as befits them, we have made the central rock motif
with more expertise: breaking, coaxing, shaping the rocks to

such wafer thinness is not always easy, but harmonized colours, sizes, shapes and 'attitudes' (ie vertical, horizontal, leaning etc) make the result well worth the effort.

From left to right, in the front, are: a lovely little Aponegeton bulb, sprouting nicely with short stems and long leaves well spread 'around the clock', ie over the 360 degrees; in the centre the spade-like Dwarf Lily covering itself with profusion; and the dual clump of *Cryptocoryne beckettii* rising higher on the right than the triangular rustic rock it obscures.

Taller plants man the back row: the plentifully propagating Malayan Sword-plant which has already multiplied its core; the towering Umbrella Fern, plain and bare of central stalk to flourish with waving ferns at the summit, reminiscent of a palm tree at an oasis; and the *Cryptocoryne willisii* to contrast its undulated, rust-coloured leaves with the fresh, green, ultra-trim *Cryptocoryne beckettii* in the front row.

The photograph above shows plants clumped round our 'Martian' rock whose futuristic tentacled mass is an original foil for some beautiful specimens: the Red Hygrophila and the smaller-leafed Green Hygrophila rising at the back; with the delicate-stemmed Red Antheria outnumbering in front the single Green Radicans, of sturdy, long leaf.

These examples show some of the basic principles of rock and plant grouping. Opposite (top to bottom) and above: Plants forming an arch *between* simple rock groups; a rugged central rock group *surrounded by* plants; a more refined rock grouping with a selection of rare plants; and the very special effect of an artificial rock arrangement, providing a fitting foil for contrasting plants.

creating an eco-system outdoors

In setting up a pond co-operation with Mother Nature is imperative, and local conditions of soil, climate, and insect life will dictate the pond you have. Florida's continuous sunshine, London's temperate changeability, and Montreal's extremes of hot/cold will decide your pond's 'balance', and hence its contents.

ponds

The *deeper* the pond, the greater your margin of error: a depth of 24"-36" inhibits freezing, the over-growth of algae, and violent fluctuations in water temperature as sun gives way to rain and cold; it will allow your plants and lilies to flourish and to compete successfully for the micro-foods on which they and the algae both live.

Also invaluable is ease of *water change*. A running spring may be an unattainable ideal, but a drain plug should be possible. This means siting the pond so that there is a slope down which the water can siphon off; access to a man-hole, a drain, a basement, any such drop in height will save much trouble later. It also means raising an immediately adjacent protective wall (6" tall or more) round the pond rim to prevent unwanted debris drifting into the water with wind and rain. If circumstances make a slope impracticable then why not buy an electric pump that can not only serve as a fountain (plus waterfall?) but can be used to empty out the pond when required; more expensive at first purchase, but a great saver of man-hours of drudgery later.

What about the *trees*? They look so lovely, but think of falling leaves. Who's going to keep cleaning out your pond, to maintain the 'balance' you had aimed for? And coupled with that, how sunny is the site you have chosen? In California long months of continuous sun will enable your plants and Lilies to out-grow the algae and out-consume the micro-foods so that the algae starve and wither; but it's very different in a changeable climate where the sun frequently alternates with cloud, because the algae are quicker off the mark initially, and can get so much more of the micro-foods that they establish themselves to the detriment of the plants.

In changeable climates then, *shade* is more helpful to the pond than is sun; the use of inhibiting chemicals, eg in spring when growth is re-starting after a harsh winter, can be judicious in restraining the quicker-spurting algae while the slower-growing plants catch up.

Intelligent co-operation with Mother Nature is the golden rule.

The same consideration applies to the *soil* in which you plan to grow your vegetation. The more hours of sun, the sooner will ferment rotting wood, festering manure, decomposing peat moss—and the more over-abundant will be hostile bacteria; in hot sun you need less artificial aids, and you'll rely more on swarming insects and air-borne spores.

In sunny conditions your *water* would tend to need changing more often, not merely because it evaporates in the heat, but because the cycles of Mother Nature's birth/growth/decay speed up, and can outrun your volume of water. Your drain plug will come in very handy now, especially if combined with a floating-ball valve (Bobby-valve is the American name) that automatically switches on the water intake if the level falls. Another partial solution is to make your pond deeper.

Now that we have focused on first things first—the laws of Mother Nature—let us then look to the details.

The more vertical *the sides*, the less the algae will tend to cling, the more they will float free in water or settle on plants. For building convenience a 2% slope is allowable, making the base only very slightly narrower than the top.

If you want sloping sides against which fish can snuggle, and sunbathe; on which marginal plants can trail and creepers daringly venture; on which insects, dragonflies, water boatmen, snails can intermingle; sloping sides that lead you into greater relationship with your pond—then you've got to pay the price: extra work, and extra shade, to cope with the extra algae; or a really good filter system, with or without changed water. These truly efficient filters exist; they are not cheap, but do give the joys of clear water.

Varying depths of water have many attractions, as your pond sides dip in organized terraces, hollows, circular levels, raised troughs; they house bog plants, and deeper-water plants: dwarf Lilies, expanding Lilies, thrusting Iris, swaying Arrowheads, clustering Marigolds, submerged forests of Elodea. You will find examples of many of these in the drawings and photographs later in the book.

But such ponds are more difficult to construct, and demand thicker cement. The often-quoted guide for a 12'×6'×2' pond-size is a 7" thick cement base tapering to 5" at the top edge; severe frosts would be better resisted by increased thicknesses, temperate climates would need less; and more complicated curves and depths would need local strengthening.

Incidentally, if you've slammed in the good old circular pond with a fountain in the middle, how are you going to clean the pond? Can you step onto the fountain? Raised troughs, tastefully arranged, can be both practical (as stepping stones or as supports for planks laid above water while cleaning, pruning or replanting) and decorative—imagine some delicate, lace-like, reed-like, soft-swaying mass just peering out of the water, isolated in the distance, alluring and attractive, certain to catch the eye of all. Imagine coloured lights playing on it; a circular fountain falling round it.

Calculating the water volume and air surface of a pond can be done with the following information. It is useful in calculating fertilizer quantities, pump capacities and so on.

The British and American gallons vary in volume:
1 Imperial (British) gallon=4.5459 litres=0.1605 cubic feet
1 United States gallon=3.785 litres=0.1339 cubic feet
1 cubic foot=28.31 litres
1 litre of water weighs 1 kilogram=1000 grams=1,000,000 milligrams

Rectangular ponds (straight sides)
British volume measurement: length×width×depth (in feet)×6.5=number of gallons
American volume measurement: length×width×depth (in feet)×7.5=number of gallons
British/US air surface: length×width (in feet)÷9=square yards of air surface

Circular ponds (straight sides)
British volume measurement: diameter×diameter×depth (in feet)×5=number of gallons

28

American volume measurement: diameter×diameter×
depth (in feet)×5.9=number of gallons
British/US air surface: $\frac{1}{2}$ diameter×$\frac{1}{2}$ diameter×3.14 (in
feet)÷9=square yards of surface

Oval ponds (straight sides)
British volume measurement: length×width×depth (in
feet)×5.9=number of gallons
American volume measurement: length×width×depth (in
feet)×6.7=number of gallons
British/US air surface: length×width (in feet)÷9=square
yards of air surface

Instant ponds are made of strengthened plastic, already
moulded, and ready to be put straight into the ground, or into
a roughly dug hollow.

Plastic pond liners are available, complete with heavy
finishers to hold down the trim-ends round the lip of the pond.

Your specialist dealer will have all manner of sizes, types,
colours, thicknesses; as well as repair kits for easily mended
(once you've found and exposed them!) leaks.

Water fountains/coloured lights are the new status symbols; they
have almost replaced the Cadillac or the Rolls-Royce parked
outside. All your neighbours can see and hear the wonderful
water-ballets, the glorious colour-fountains, the jets ever
changing sizes and heights, flooded with coloured lights that
phase from white, to red, to purple, to gold; splashing,
cascading, flowing over water-falls, emanating from
gargoyle-heads, from the faces (or elsewhere!) of cherubs; in
circular shapes, in towering upreach, in wide-spread curtains.

Improved technology has made it possible to indulge your
taste. You could do well to remember that the higher the jet the
more area the splash will affect; it really is surprising how far
spray can be carried by even moderate winds. Stories of
passers-by in the street being made wet by over-ambitious
displays have been known.

The simple jet fountain and the single submerged light are
also popular; are simply and cheaply installed; and are often
transformed down to only 12 volts for special safety. They can
readily be incorporated into a plastic-moulded or a plastic-lined
pond, as well as the cement-lined type.

Water re-circulation serves a purpose practical in the extreme
as an inhibitor of stagnation. In hot, thundery weather the
oxygen content of the water lessens, and a fountain spray can
actually save fish lives. Plants and Lilies seem to find the gentle

under-surface level circulation of current helpful in cross-fertilization as well as in clearing areas that might otherwise fester.

Dry climates, in which water-evaporation tends to expose the soil and so to harm the plants, can be countered by burying 6″ below soil level some plastic tubing profusely punctured so that water played through it in dry weather gets to the roots first, rather than just dampening the soil surface.

In emergencies a hollow tube could be inserted vertically to penetrate down several inches and water could be made to percolate slowly out to the roots. Even a long-necked bottle could be thrust neck downwards to allow water to permeate below surface level.

The planting medium should contain about 20% fertilizer to 80% soil, when plants are the main emphasis. Positively no insecticides should be used in the fertilizer, preferably none even in the surrounding garden; and the hotter the sun the less the quantity required, and the greater the danger from fermentation/decomposition.

Please note: all waters vary; the enormous variety of foreign bodies that get blown in, carried in, dissolved in, makes a precise prediction of chemical reaction difficult.

When adding chemicals or medicines or fertilizers it could be prudent to introduce half only of the suggested dose at first; then to add the two remaining quarter doses, spaced apart (for 24 hours?), if no unusual reaction is being produced.

choice of plants

Floating plants provide much needed shadow if you want to cut down the sunlight (in a changeable climate) striking the water surface, and activating the quicker-growing algae.

Submerged plants of many lovely shades of light or dark green soon grow forest-like as they expand their clusters.

Many owners prefer to plant in pots: pond-cleaning is easier; plants can be re-positioned, pruned and eliminated the more readily. A sand covering of 1″ deep should protect the soil in the pot, which should either be 'big enough' or have slotted exits through which roots can expand.

If fish tend to eat the plants (because you are giving wrong, monotonous or irregular food) then galvanized netting held in a cone some 6″ away from plant growth can be a protection.

Lilies are of literally hundreds of varieties, some of which are photographed later in the book. Perhaps the main classifications are the hardy, special, annual, and tuber Lilies, and finally the 'changers'.

The hardy Lilies can stand most depths (12–36″) and will send their runners to the water surface so that the leaves expand there.

The specials demand pre-stated depths, and insist that you lift them up to an exact level so that their leaves float naturally.

The annuals grow and grow. These can be hived off to make new Lilies. They should be fertilized annually.

A tuber, the banana-like long 'root' of a Lily, should be planted horizontally, not upright, at a slope of 2″ off level, and at a comfortable depth of 4–8″ dependent on type. If a young shoot is already emerging from the tuber, then leave the shootlet just exposed above the soil.

The changers are Lily blooms that change with the light, so that some bloom during noon, others at dusk; some actually alter their very colour with waxing or waning light.

Marginal plants grow in shallow water 1–8″ deep round the edges, and provide shelter for all manner of small life (both air and water borne); Water Mint, Water Cress, Water Creepers all stay of minimum height; Water Violet and dozens more grow to 6–12″; Water Iris, Arrowheads, Rush, Reeds and the like can tower up 36″. Some of these appear later, in the photographs. For further information you should consult any good gardening book.

indoor plants and display

Beauty and Joy are yours for the effort, fortunately not too much effort, and with endless scope for variety. We give now twelve colour plates as examples of what can be created, using one tank per room, or several tanks in the one room; for the office, the bedroom, the lounge or the hall; for public places like cocktail bars, shop displays, medical waiting rooms.

All twelve are original designs. To the best of our knowledge there are none now in existence quite like them. However, for decades past, our artists here in the heart of London's fashionable West End have been pioneering new materials, new arrangements, new combinations. Our tanks crowd the homes of the rich, the distinguished, as well as the popular and the widespread.

Plants feature loud and clear. Fish are definitely subsidiary and are mentioned only incidentally.

Plants are often identified by name, pinpointed by scientific nomenclature. Yet many are the varieties local to your own home town that can, and should, be used—these we have 'symbolised' by using plastic reproductions of plants, indicative of the vast varieties found round the planet, often with differing names, and we urge that you experiment, you try, you innovate. Similarly with rocks—provided you follow the guidelines mentioned earlier, you should make imaginative use of the varieties available to you locally.

Earnestly we hope the Beauty and Joy are yours.

Opposite: An attractive aquarium group; most prominent are typical Cryptocoryne bog plants.

colour harmony

Eye-catching, this layout demands instant attention, as befits a restaurant, a cocktail bar, a shop, or any such public place where people have no previous intention of viewing a fish tank, and where you want to stop them in their tracks and force them to look.

High colour is essential. Our rocks are of an extreme beauty, featuring a veined effect both in the yellow (which is pure Italian crystal from Venice, and not merely glass) and in the exquisite white quartz from a little-known quarry in Wiltshire, England. Care has been taken to site this on blue sand of varying consistency and shade, while leaving the red sand in one single tone, which helps to sharpen the effect of the towering, thin peak placed in it. Your local rocks are sure to be usable if you follow the above principles.

The plants have deliberately been bunched round the veined quartz rock to allow its whiteness to 'peer' through, and to soften the colours; they provide quiet and shelter for the timid fish, and give predominance to the strikingly firm, dark plant (the Cryptocoryne). In fact, we have emphasised the point here by siting two strong specimens side by side. To lead the eye back into the glare of the red area we have placed a softer green Cryptocoryne plant on the 'edge' of the yellow crystal, leaving the arresting colour-contrast beauty to pole-axe you.

Here, you can site your favourite 'objet d'art' or allow a few strong fish to swarm, and flash their fins. Note how the stepped-back pieces of yellow crystal have horizontal veining to sharpen the effect and to encourage your eye to travel back into the far distance; and so to increase the impression of roominess from front to back.

The soft blue of the background, inviting calm, is a clear contrast with the blue of the sand and the crystals.

Plants: 1 Ludwigia, 2 Myriophyllum, 3 Hygrophila, 4 artificial, 5 Vallisneria, 6 Elodea, 7 Cryptocoryne, 8 Cabomba. Rocks: A English crystal, B Venetian crystal, C Wiltshire quartz. *Note:* tank plan shows view from above.

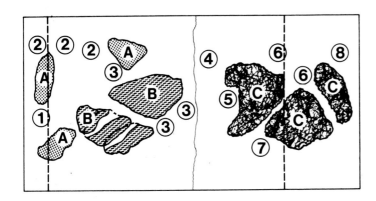

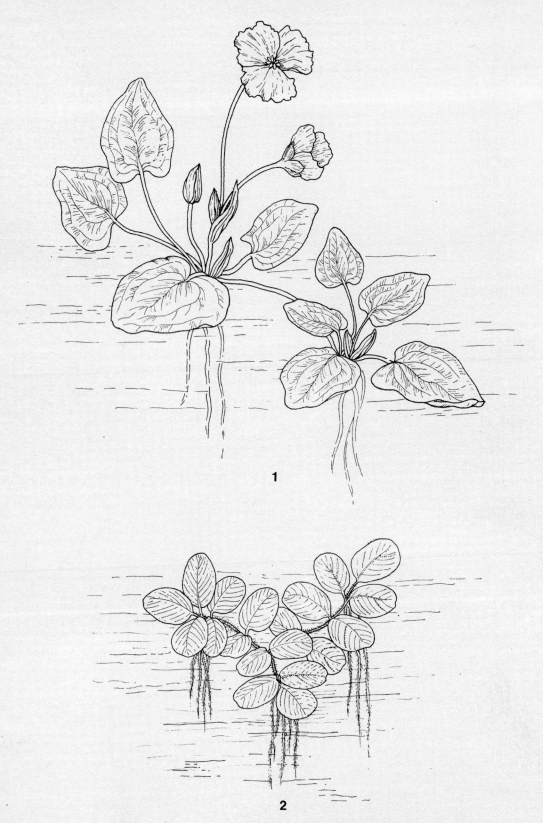

1

2

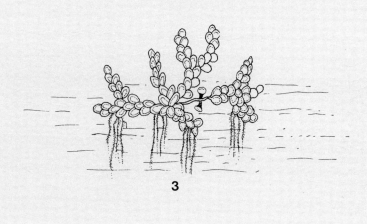

3

4

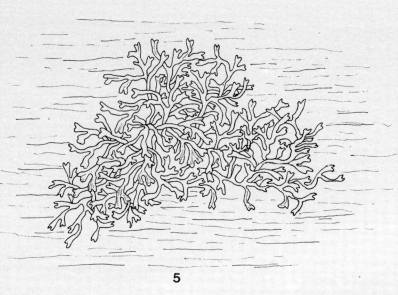

5

These cut down excess light, and help increase acidity; short roots reach down towards but not touching soil.

1
Hydrocharis Morsus-ranae blooms readily and reduces alkalinity.
2
Salvinia auriculata often forms chainlike extensions when expanding; dies in winter; thrives in light and warmth; likes to reach for soil.
3
Azolla caroliniana can have a reddish tinge in summer; likes light and dies in winter; tolerates most pond or aquarium waters.
4
Lemna minor, tiny, bright green, can be used as fish food; found on ponds everywhere.
5
Riccia fluitans is a lovely, clear green, flourishing in poor light; very popular for aquaria.

rising cliffs

A display designed for a typical, fairly tall tank of household size, 24"×12", and 24" deep, highlighting the following features:

The most prominent is a single, strong central motif made of a large middle tier with a dual superstructure of brilliant white coral of futuristic upreaching effect.

It serves also as a very tall protective cave into and onto which any fish you may add can swim or cling.

It is flanked by towering cliffs that would screen the heaters/filters/thermometers etc, and contrast clearly but not too strikingly with the totally different rocks of the central tier. Their grand reach is nearly the whole, 24" height of the tank.

The plant life then is as a screen behind, around, below, in front, topped off with a strong red coral, deliberately off-centred, and balanced by the red plants, the blue plants, the striped green-and-white plants; the eye moves naturally from right to left to front.

Plant contrasts will subtly create quiet harmony.

The coral area is tall, lush and exuberant, softened by the delicate light green whorls (of the Cabomba) with a totally different hard, tough dark green leaf thrusting through the background gap, then—nothing: only rock cliff, gleaming dull red (so very different from the bright, light, aerated red of the coral).

By contrast, the left-hand side of the aquascape is bare of strong motif. Here quietness reigns, and you can enjoy the soft delicate whorls of the tall Cabomba. The front as a whole left-to-right is relatively clear, as the tiered arch is placed some way back. It features the unusual plants. It leaves open space for contrast. The sand is of differing consistencies, very apt to catch the light, unlike the sky-blue background withdrawing into the distance.

Plants: 1 Ivy rush, 2 Sagittaria, 3 Cryptocoryne, 4 Bacopa, 5 Cabomba, 6 Anubias, 7 artificial, 8 Vallisneria. Rocks: A Somerset, B White coral, C Welsh slate, D black Devon, E red coral. *Note:* tank plans show view from above; upper level shown on right.

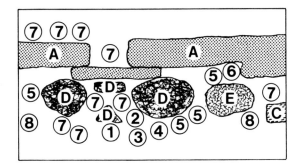

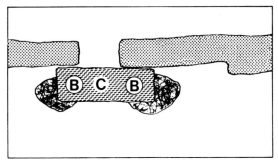

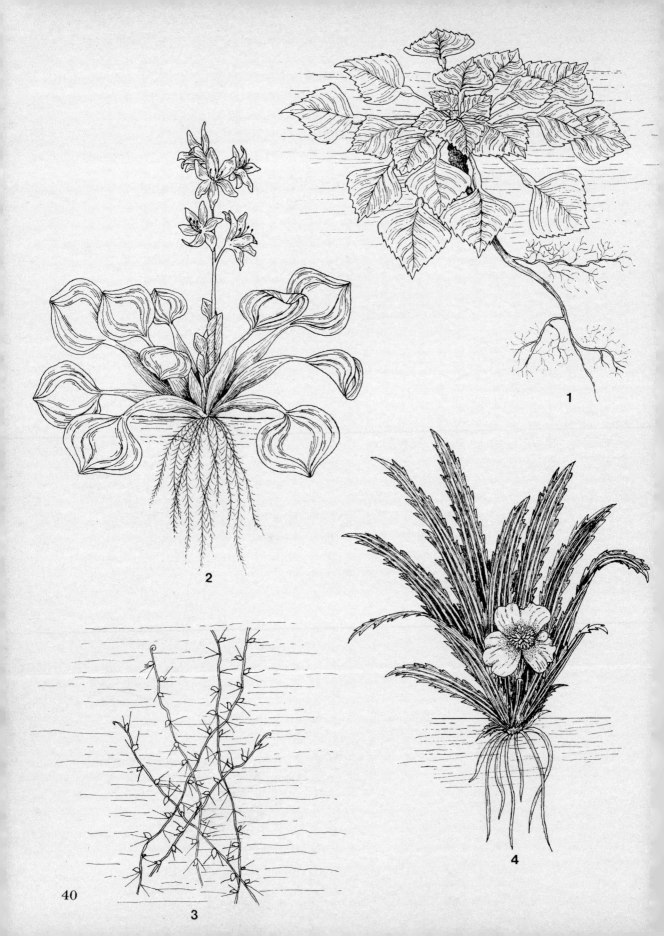

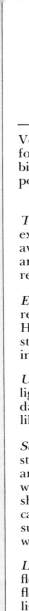

Very positive root formations; suitable for bigger tanks and warm ponds.

1
Trapa natans is very expansive, and widely available; acidity, warmth and light bring out red/purple tinges.

2
Eichhornia crassipes resembles a land Hyacinth, its roots stretching down 36"; dies in winter.

3
Utricularia exoleta has tiny, light-green stems with darker green swellings; likes light and acid water.

4
Stratiotes aloides has leaves striped brown and dark and light green, blooms white and yellow; likes shelter and warm water; can grow to 18"; thrives in summer and dies in winter.

5
Limnobium spongia is flecked green with a white flower; likes soft water, light and warmth; fine for tanks and ponds; dies in winter.

6
Pistia stratiotes grows as light-green rosettes 2-6" across, with blue roots; hates draughts, needs pH 6.8 (acid), warmth and light; dies in winter.

7
Utricularia vulgaris consumes small aquatic life such as daphnia; cold, acid water brings out the yellow/green of the leaves, and the rust/yellow of the flower.

5

6

7

underwater forest

A beautiful underwater forest scene with lush vegetation, with stone combining with wood, with two-tier structure, with gleaming white sand; a whiteness carried through in the superb rocks from Devon—all giving grandeur of height, especially if the tank is placed slightly above eye-level. Notice the subsidiary lighting peering through from behind, just sufficiently strong to prevent any feeling of darkness that a forest can sometimes impart, and to bring the uplifting sense of peace/repose that can fulfil and calm instead.

Aeration bubbles in a delicate swirling rise can be made to 'drip upwards' as they bounce from deep inside the recess of the central cave, streaming from rock to leaf to surface.

Just enough colour is provided by the plants on the central arch to contrast with the white-veined rocks and to suggest exotic tropical flowers; the towering red hue of the plant immediately behind adds to the pleasant sense of joy.

The contrast of the soft bark, maturing in the water and harbouring all manner of micro-organisms which Mother Nature will spawn thereon, and of the strongly gaunt cliff-like rocks as though bathed in sunshine, as can happen in a forest clearing, is quietly arresting. We had thought of splattering the white sand with reddish tints for those who prefer more colour, but in the end left the few darkened specks instead to bring out the white even more.

Your plants will grow tall, and be encouraged to flower in such a setting; the tank is only 18″ long and 24″ high but looks much, much more. If your room is small and squat, then this 'underwater forest' is ideal for you.

Plants: 1 Cabomba, 2 Elodea, 3 Hygrophila, 4 artificial. Rocks and other features: A bark, B red Mendip, C special quartzed black Devon, D Mendip slate. *Note:* tank plan shows view from above.

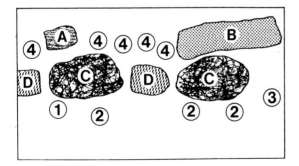
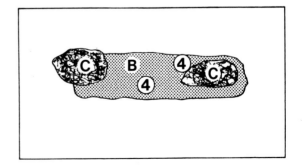

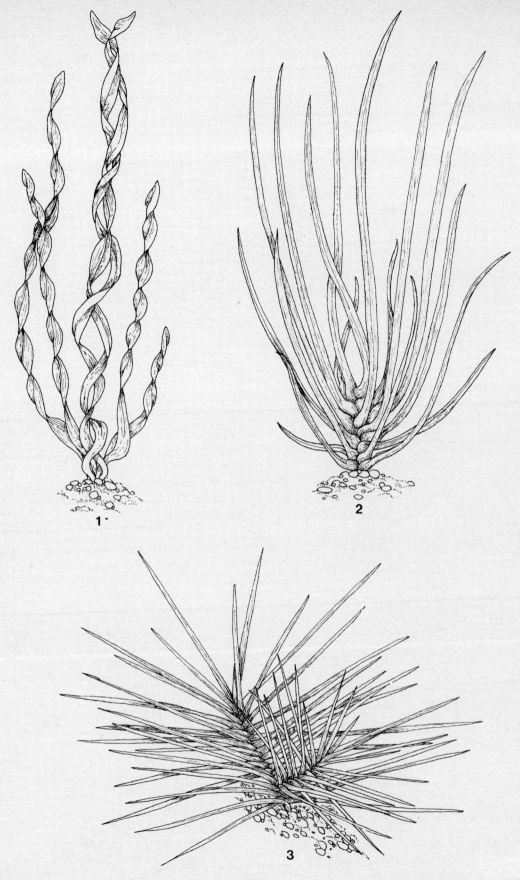

1

2

3

44

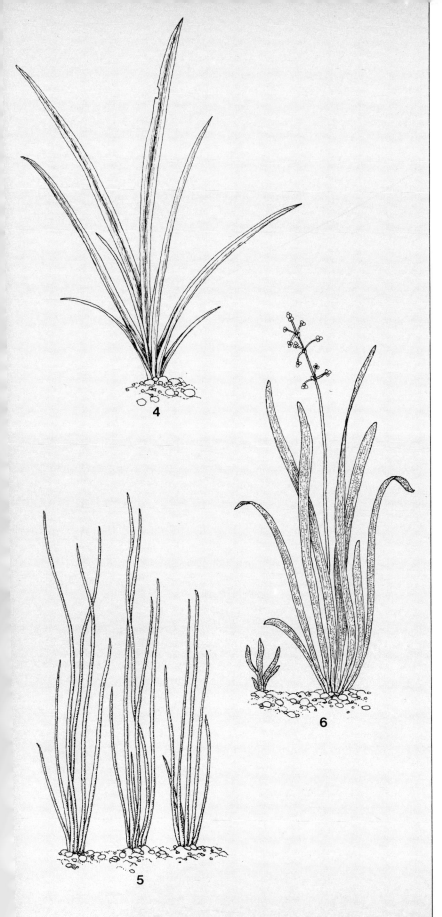

grass-like, tough perennials

When planting do not cover the crown (where the white of the roots shades into the green of the leaves).

1
Vallisneria spiralis forma portugalensis is a more 'corkscrewed' version of ever-popular 'twisted vallis', with two tones of green; hardy and grows to 18″.

2
Acorus calamus, typical of genus, can grow up to 20″, stiff and tall with prominent rootstock; grows anywhere in temperatures down to 63°F.

3
Acorus gramineus tends to stay short in lovely green clumps; hardy, and can even take 63°F; propagates quickly over prominent root stock.

4
Ivory rush, recently very popular, has bright green leaves with white trims; hardy and slow-growing, but can attain 7-10″.

5
Eleocharis acicularis is minute, slim and green; it is difficult to plant, but hardy once established; makes superb carpet of slender, thread-like undulations.

6
Sagittaria subulata forma pusilla has ribbonlike leaves wider than Vallisneria, with 3-veined vertical division in each leaf; colouring a flecked green; a hardy, popular choice.

executive office

This heavily planted, two-tier, subdued design is ideal for the quiet room with antique or period furniture, where the tank will be viewed at fairly close range. August Chairmen/Presidents/dignitaries will find it irresistibly imposing.

In their quiet but compelling way, the subtle-toned rocks are magnificent: the huge, towering Mendip slate at the rear, in two great slabs that dominate all, defying time and mulm as their powerful hues and stratification attract attention. Increasing attention. The longer you are in their company the more you will be susceptible to their inner confidence—just like the august Chairman whose desk they should adorn.

The arch is also of the same slate, but the infrastructure below is of lovely Devon rock with its whiter-than-white veins and of Welsh slate in prosaic form deliberately placed below so as not to challenge the august Mendip; both are all but screened by plants to give privacy and also softened contours.

An impudent piece has somehow sneaked onto the august arch: a cheap, pretty, ordinary, partly hidden, curvaceous shell—cute in its off-angle balance so that a tiny fish could wriggle in at the bottom and hide inside; to join a more patrician Venetian crystal, 'mustard' in tone, rather upward-pointed and hard-lined—that you overlook at your peril.

The sand is very special, a million-hued flint, wide-ranging and sparkling and ever catching the light—as befits the far-flung ramifications of the august, at the very seat of power, magnetic and strong.

Plants: 1 Cabomba, 2 Bacopa, 3 Myriophyllum, 4 Aponogeton, 5 Vallisneria, 6 artificial. Rocks: A Mendip slate, B Devon, C shell, D Venetian crystal. *Note:* tank plans show view from above; upper level shown on right.

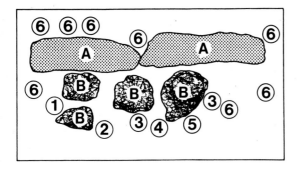

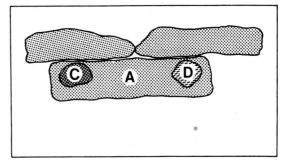

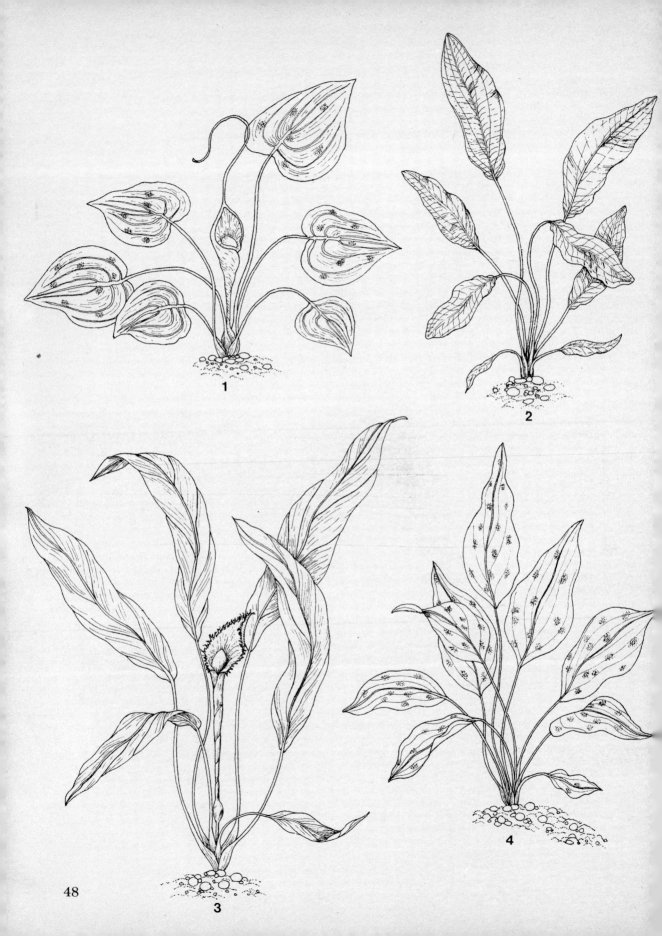

1

2

3

4

48

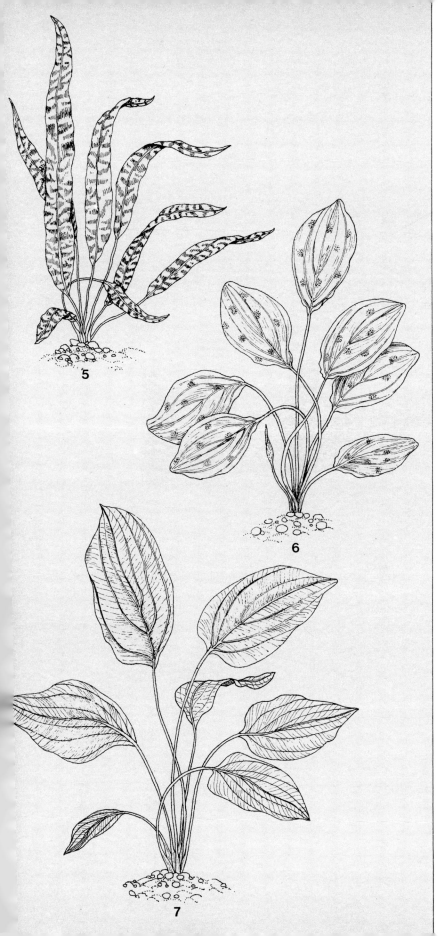

These root slowly, shedding leaves early, may emerse.

1
Cryptocoryne johorensis has spade-shaped leaves of a medium green, slightly corrugated, with dark-brown smudges and symmetrical veining.

2
Cryptocoryne beckettii is hardy and purple throughout (older leaves darker); flower has purple dots on white tubular growth.

3
Cryptocoryne ciliata grows up to 20″; two-tone leaves with central rib, crossed with 6 veins; yellow tinge suggests sulking flower.

4
Cryptocoryne grandis has very dark leaf with almost-black markings around central rib; can grow to 25″ tall.

5
Cryptocoryne balansae has light leaves with heavy darker-green corrugations; crisp edges often fray below 78°F; can grow to 25″.

6
Cryptocoryne blassii has purple-red base shading to red-brown edges, yellow-brown flecks between yellow-green veining.

7
Cryptocoryne cordata has dark-green leaves on purple stems; older leaves go red-purple before being shed; prefers 78-84°F; tolerates most waters, but prefers them soft and slightly acid.

beginner's set-up

A simple, practical design, for the owner who is just starting, and who has only one tank. The colour is amply spattered and varied, and gives the beauty and thrill that the novice will demand; and the protective, dark, overhanging tree bark will help keep the quality of the water (its pH) correct, as well as making a serviceable contrast. The blue background harmonizes with the multi-million hues of the (rather special) flint of the base, gently sloped left-to-right and slightly back-to-front.

Plants soften the overall effect, and have been placed in clumps as if by a novice aquarist. All are readily available, quick to root and to bush, and yet are modestly priced. The foreground has been left free to encourage movement there, and the really thick protection of the leaves has been based under and behind the tree bark.

Such a design is eminently suitable if you are frequently experimenting with your tank, are often cleaning it, replacing plants, and so on; yet it looks good. Your friends will admire it. The basic rhythm is that of pairs. We have stepped the three blood-red rocks backwards into the far distance, and paired them with one largish red rock on the front right, nicely veined to pick up the colour of the yellow one behind, also veined, and paired with the similar-but-different yellow one holding fort in the centre left. A delightful criss-cross of colour, of veining, of contrast, of position—which between them 'make' your tank. The turquoise (note its soft aerated composition) and quite different other purple-blue pairs complete the contrast; one squat/tall, the other horizontal/tapering. In the midst of all this, the tree bark stands out even more.

Plants: 1 Vallisneria, 2 Bacopa, 3 Ludwigia, 4 Myriophyllum. Rocks and other features: A English crystal, B Venetian crystal, C bark. *Note:* tank plan shows view from above.

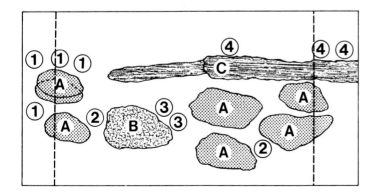

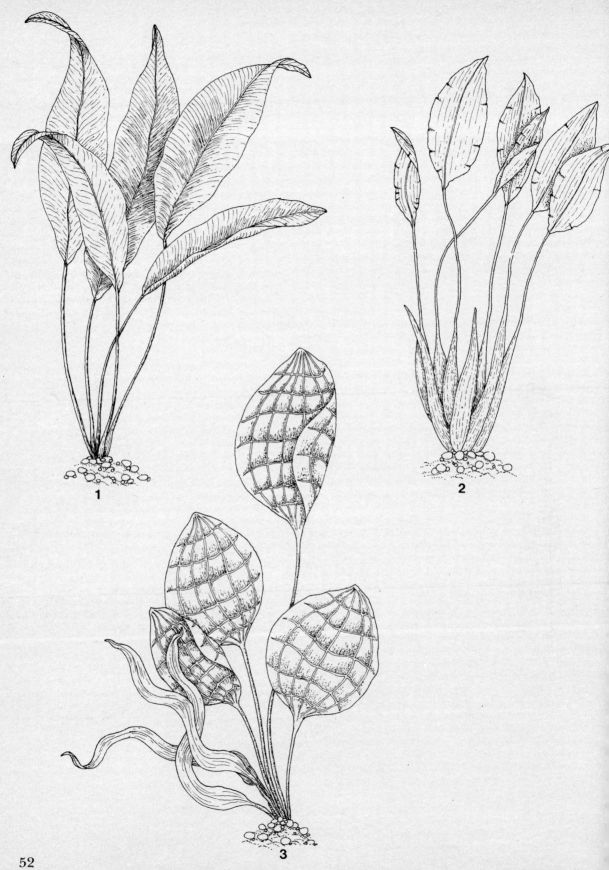

1

2

3

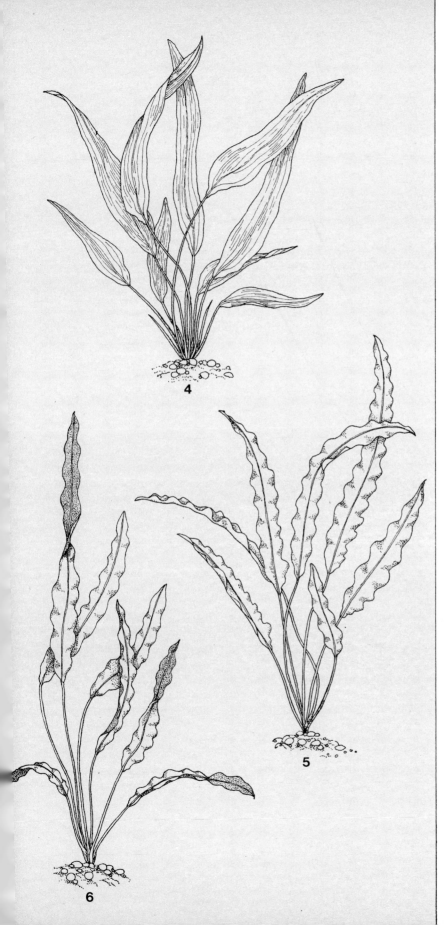

Hardy favourites for aquaria/ponds, tending to emerse. Tough leaves shelter micro-organisms, good for tank balance. Allow 4″ soil depth for roots.

1

Anubias congensis grows to 10″; needs 77-85°F, and bright light; tough, dark-green leaves with prominent central rib, and stems yellow-green.

2

Lagenandra ovata can emerse to 30″, given thick, rich soil, underwater and emersent leaves differ (older ones go purple before shedding).

3

Ottelia alismoides has ribbon-like underwater leaves, which change on emersing; rich soil maintains the light green—pH 6.8, DH 3-6, 73-9°F.

4

Cryptocoryne nevilii is very tough bottle-green plant preferring soft, rich soil and strong light; emerses readily outdoors.

5

Cryptocoryne undulata ever popular, has rounded base to a green, wrinkled leaf, which goes purple before shedding; leaves, which will grow to 3″, broaden and darken when emersent.

6

Cryptocoryne willisii, another favourite, has slightly yellow green leaf, undulating, with prominent central rib; here too leaves go purple before shedding and broaden when emersent.

temple ruin

Have you ever seen a temple ruin on sand, bare all round except for a few rocks essential to maintain its structure? The inescapable contrast of the towering base slopes and of the surmounting rock-pile has not been captured by our camera but is easy to visualize. Such a design is functional in the extreme as all dirt, mulm, and plant debris tend to fall downwards to the base edges of the tank floor, and are easily siphoned off.

Your plants will smile happily as they bask bang under the top light, without even having to bother to stretch upwards. That is why we have put in 'ordinary' rather untidy plants, 'unimpressive' except for the one magnificent ivy leaf that stands proudly out, and offers shade from its strong leaves.

The rock is gorgeously stratified, mellowed with white veins accentuating its subdued but unforgettable red glow. The background 'brings forward' the colour to remind the poetic of

a sunset. The sand is coarser than often is usual, but glitters unmistakably in its multi-tone consistencies and spatters the horizontal slabs as your fish swirl past.

At first sight, this 'tor rock', which comes from the beautifully coloured Esterel Mountains guarding the South of France's Riviera coast, is not as eye-catching as the Venetian crystal and Wiltshire quartz on page 34, but very quickly grows on you in the calm of your room. The delicacy of the shades will increasingly become apparent and will even seem to reflect the bright/vivid/living colours of your own ornaments, which could strikingly be placed in that quiet area to the extreme right where the best plants are stationed: short, stocky Ludwigia in front, the powerfully robust ivy leaf as the central bastion, and the tall flowering Cabomba in the rear almost sweeping the water surface.

See tank plan and key, p. 58.

55

1

2

3

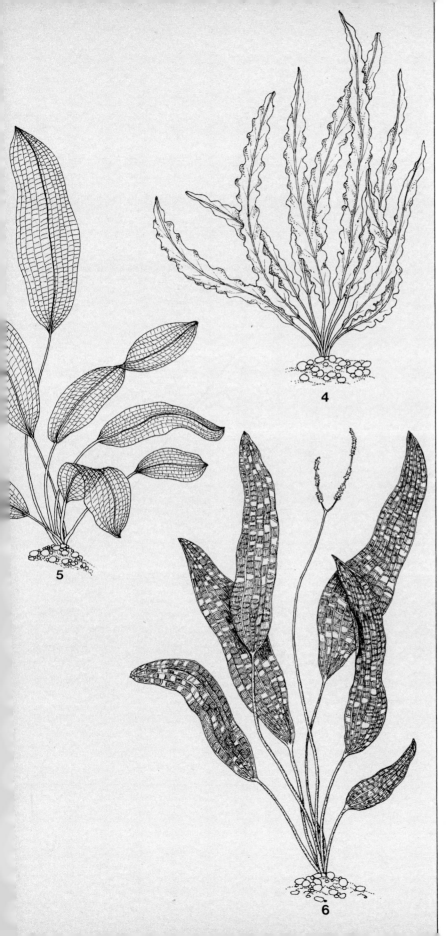

Aponogetons

Not too difficult to grow, they demand cleaner and bigger tanks than some plants and adequate light.

1
Aponogeton ulvaceus has curvaceous, almost floppy leaves with dark green centre shading to bright green; can grow to more than 20".

2
Aponogeton elongatus is dark green and surprisingly hardy; can emerse to 24", and produce fluffy yellow flower; shallow, soft, acid water and 78°F with rich soil cause leaf to shorten and widen.

3
Aponogeton crispus is a beautiful pale green, but much less delicate than it looks; can emerse, and produce white flower.

4
Aponogeton undulatus has crispate, undulating leaves, dark green round the centre rib and shading to yellow-green at edges; hardy and can grow to 8".

5
Aponogeton fenestralis (Madagascar lace plant) hates draughts and demands clear water with pH 6.8, 74-80°F, DH 3-6; given space can grow to 30"; algae or mulm clog its lace-like leaves.

6
Aponogeton bernieranus is another 'lace plant', also from Madagascar, shorter, tougher, darker and less regular in its nervations; when emersent may produce double-spiked flowers of gorgeous rose/white.

Plan for 'temple ruin', pp. 54-5.
Plants: 1 Myriophyllum, 2 Cabomba, 3 Ivy leaf, 4 Ludwigia. Rocks: all from the Esterel Mountains in the South of France. *Note:* tank plan shows view from above.

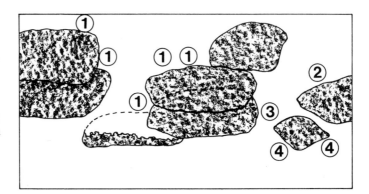

outer space

According to your temperament: merely garish or stunning! Calling to mind futuristic, entwining flows of energy, from the year 2000, this is our 'Martian' rock: the plants are all of plastic, in arresting hues. You won't be able to take your (delighted or horrified) eyes off it.

Eminently suitable for a large fish tank that is viewed from a distance, the arrangement should be placed in a large hall, room or lobby, where a broad, sweeping panorama is called for, rather than the minute finesse of a close-up. The only concession we've made to planet Earth is the common-or-garden sand—all else is 'outer space'.

Please do be ultra-careful to provide genuinely fast-flow power filtration, otherwise those same crannies could become festering backwaters of decaying debris. Our filters are all (three!) housed at the rear, kept from abutting onto the blue glass of the tank back, and the filtered water is sprayed in (hidden) jets TOWARDS the front of the tank thus washing into view any debris. You'll love to see your fish diving into these strong (yet invisible) streams of water and playing follow-my-leader as they swim against the tide.

For photographic reasons, we did not add here streaming air bubbles, escaping from the innumerable gaps and air holes of the Martian rock, nor too is reproduced the soothing therapeutic melody that such aerated-all-over water sounds, like a miniature, hushed and distant water-fountain. Just the thing to soothe a headache, and to encourage calm, meditative thought—even in a big hall!

Colours could be increased or softened by a change of lighting, which could be phased to vary not only in intensity, but also to pinpoint or to diffuse. It could even be made to shine out from behind.

Plants: all artificial. Rocks: 'Martian'—that is, plastic extrusions to our own specifications. *Note:* tank plans show view from above; upper level on right.

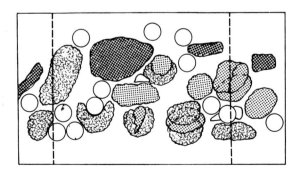

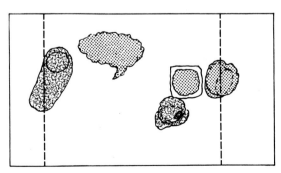

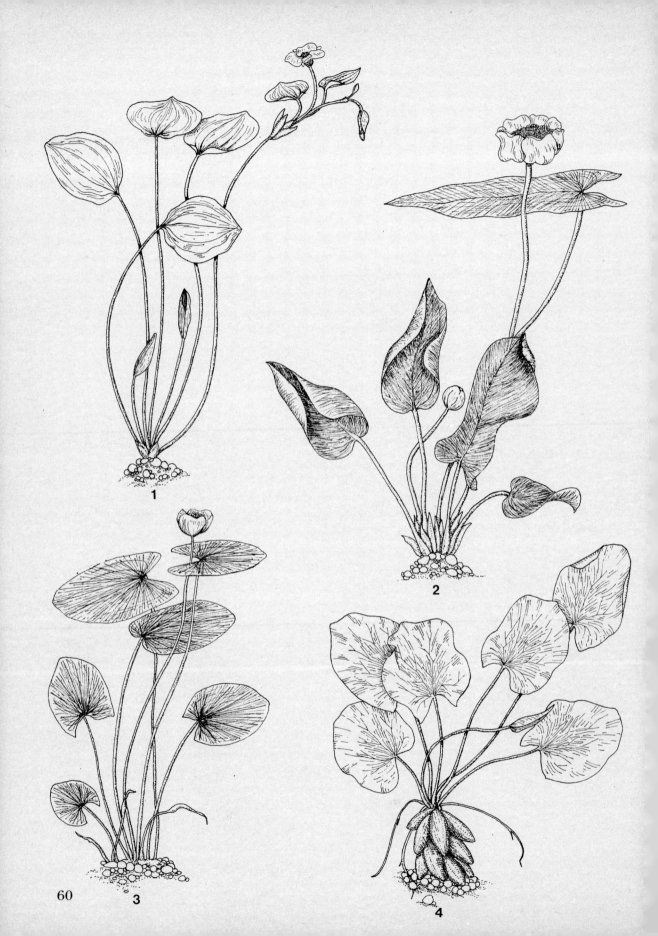

1

2

3

4

Except for the banana plant, all can be grown in tank or pond, and are increasingly popular.

1
Hydrocleis nymphaeoides has fine heart-shaped leaves and yellow flower; adverse conditions restrict it to some 8″, with curled, dark-green leaves.

2
Nuphar luteum has floppy, yellow-green leaves with yellow-brown flowers; floating leaves strong and flat; ideal conditions 55-65°F, pH 6.8, DH 8.

3
Nuphar pumillum, small pond Lily increasingly used in larger tanks; grows to 20″ with dark green leaves and yellow flowers; likes chalky soil and lower temperatures.

4
Nymphaeoides aquatica (Banana Plant, from its roots) is native to the USA; leaves vary from yellow-green to purple.

5
Sagittaria sagittifolia, commonly found in USA, can grow to 30″ in very deep tank; leaves dark green and flower, when present, white/violet; may wither in winter.

6
Sagittaria montividensis is shorter than *S. sagittifolia*, with darker leaves and cream/purple flower.

7
Sagittaria guyanensis can reach 25″, but 10″ is common; developing leaves change from oval to kidney in shape, and darken to olive green; emersent leaves start erect, then flop over to float.

hermit's cave

Ever been to the Nilgiri hills in India and seen the dozens upon dozens of caves of the 'Holy Men' stacked into the mountain sides? We've reproduced the principle of separate compartments in which you could keep otherwise incompatible fish (like a whole range of cichlids) or a display of personal ornaments or mementoes distributed each in their own place. We have illustrated the idea here with plant-blooms.

The stepping-up, layer upon layer, rising to the full height and then 'almost being lost in the distance' can be very effective indeed, both for fish and for ornaments or plants. Deliberately we have played the lighting down onto the front and lower echelons, so as to leave contrasting 'gloom rising into distance'; and have accentuated this further by slightly highlighting the corners while maintaining the centre shrouded. Such a picture is very easy to live with, and will give height to a squat room, especially when placed just above eye-level.

We have indicated the 'steep and narrow path of enlightenment', as you climb from the bottom-left to the top-right, where the spherical all-encompassing blue flower welcomes you.

All the rocks are natural, and man-made colours have been avoided. Only the sand is free-flowing, in direct contrast to the rigidities above. Yet the interweaving of dull slate, flat and prosaic with the rising veins of the quartz rocks, and with the looming 'mountain' in the centre-top background, all gives a restrained yet fascinating effect that grows on you the more you study it. It is very easy to live with, and like the set-up on page 42 will give height to a squat room, especially when placed just above eye-level.

If you enthuse about plants and can mature fine blooms you can use these terraces and steps to effect a magnificent display. If necessary you could grow the plants in separate pots (with specialist soil or manure) concealed thereon. Strong filtration would probably be advisable in this case, and you could use the flow of water emerging from your filters to sway the large rounded leaves in the top centre, making them 'ring like holy gongs/bells' to focus the thoughts of all who enter your home.

See tank plan and key, p. 66.

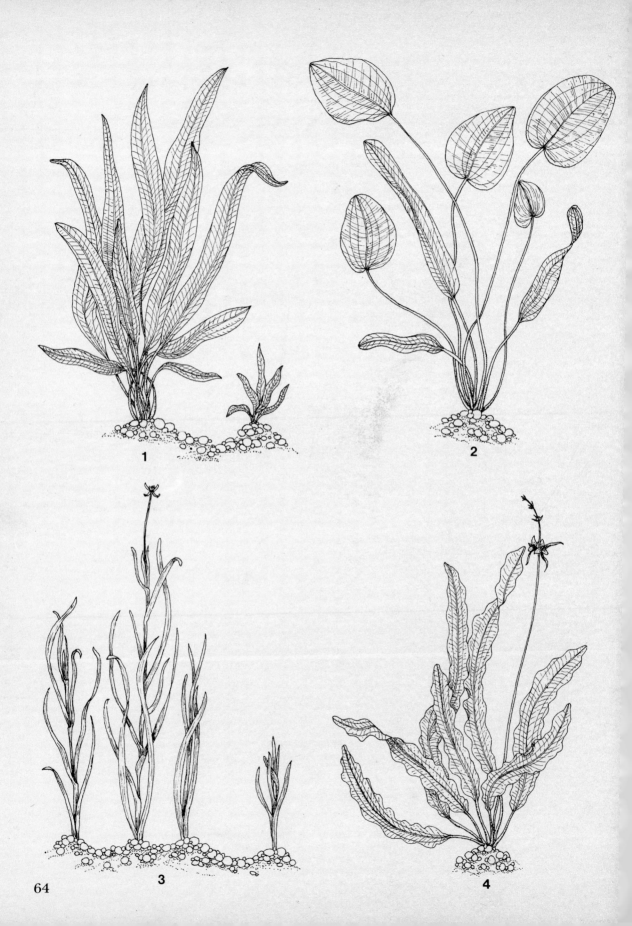

1

2

3

4

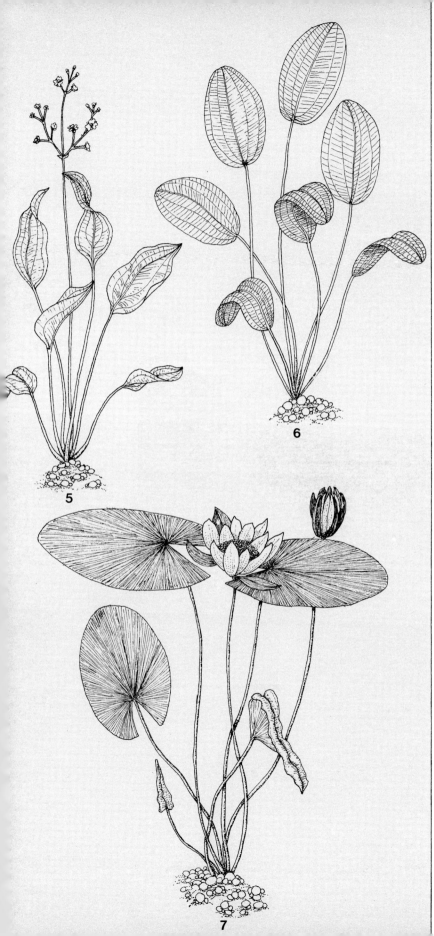

5

6

7

For the focus of an indoor tank, or warmed (indoor) pond.

1
Echinodorus brevipedicellatus has light-green leaves growing to 12-18″.

2
Echinodorus berteroi grows to 30″; young ribbon leaves develop to oval, or even heart-shape.

3
Heterantha dubia behaves variably—leaves sometimes stay stumpy under water, sometimes float, outdoors sometimes emerse to 70″; prefers 70-80°F and pH 7.2, but will tolerate 50°F in winter and up to 7.9.

4
Echinodorus martii is Brazilian in origin; better the conditions the more lush and light green the leaves; blue and white flowers will shoot up to 24″ above the water given space.

5
Echinodorus cordifolius, an American swamp plant, is slightly prickly to touch; can grow to 70″, but 12″ quite normal.

6
Echinodorus longistylus has thrusting, tough, dark green leaves that emerse to 20″ outdoors; propagated by living rootstock, which should be fleshy.

7
Nymphaea alba is a typical water lily for the tank; clusters of yellow/white flowers appear among top-floating leaves; lighter the green, the happier.

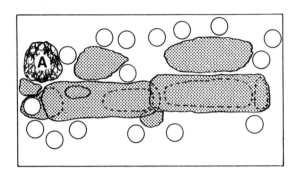

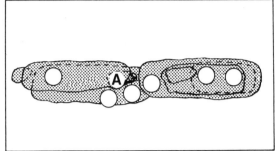

Plan for 'hermit's cave', p. 62.
Plants: all artificial. Rocks:

A quartzed Wiltshire, remainder Mendip slate. *Note:* tank plans show view

from above; upper level shown on right.

ƒantasia

Colour, movement, light and gaiety all tumble over each other in this dramatic effect which is virtually guaranteed to stop the passer-by and to make him look at your tank, be this in the corridor, the entrance-hall, the shop, the bar, or the waiting-room.

Fundamental to the display, and unfortunately not to be photographed, are (1) movement, as the balls are made to spin and to sway in the jets of water emerging from filters; (2) lights which flash as the multi-faceted spheres reflect them; this will particularly be so if phased lighting is used to ring the changes between evenly diffused and sharply focused rays, with or without the intermittent pause of darkness, plus or minus changing colours of the light itself; (3) air bubbles that dance and rebound and colour and burst in swirling masses.

Only the rounded block in the centre front and the contrasting rear block will remain stationary; all the rest will move/laugh/kaleidoscope. You'll stand open-mouthed, riveted to the ever-changing scene. It'll make your party go with a swing, but go!

Can you imagine the superb ripples of excitement you would achieve if you were to place four of these units in the four corners of a room and then turn off the remaining lights?

Stereoscopic disco lighting and other teenage joys would pale into insignificance for one big reason—these lights/colours/movements softened by being emanated through water are most flattering—yes, flattering! Everyone 'aged 21 and over' will respond to that.

Plants: 1 Hygrophila, 2 artificial, 3 Ludwigia, 4 Ambulia, 5 Ivy leaf. Rocks and other features: A multi-faceted glass sphere, B quartzed Mendip, C English crystal. *Note:* tank plan shows view from above.

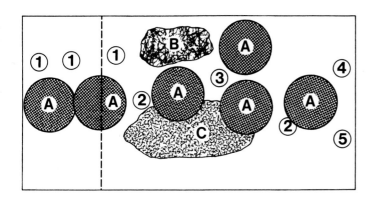

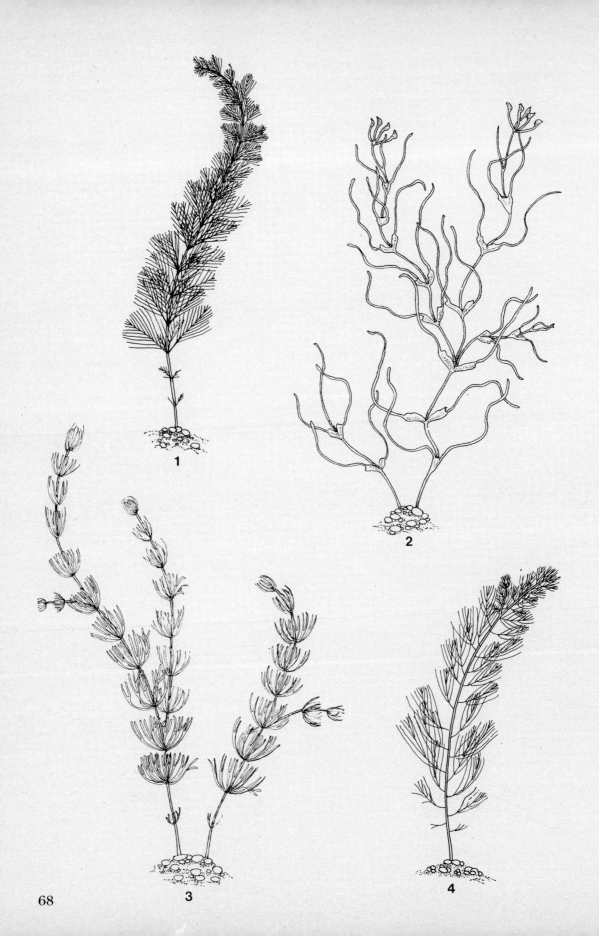

68

1

2

3

4

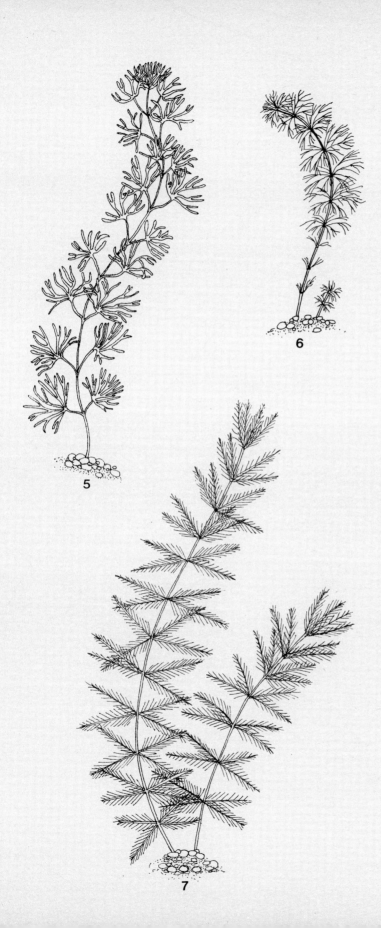

These all grow to the surface, and then trail; look best in clumps.

1
Myriophyllum spicatum has leaves wine-red underneath in Nature; under cultivation, warm red tint covers whole plant.

2
Ruppia maritima is rare and multiplies by filiform leaves; notice how nodes thicken to shoot out more growth; pH 7–7.5 preferred.

3
Ceratophyllum demersum, favourite for pond and tank, prefers 45-64°F; fast growing, needing rich soil.

4
Myriophyllum verticillatum is dense and lush, with dark green, softly undulating foliage.

5
Cabomba aquatica is great favourite, with beautifully whorled spheres round delicately waving central stem; hardy, but ideal conditions are good light, pH 6.8, DH 8, 76°F; goes slimy if over-hot.

6
Ambulia heterophylla is very popular with light green whorls clustered into rosettes; resembles Cabomba, but smaller and darker; goes slimy over 82°F.

7
Myriophyllum elatinoides is more typical Myriophyllum, more feathery and lighter-green, at best about 15″.

children's fairy ring

It's fairy land, so the sky is pink and the soil is blue; old-man Gnome sits in the middle of his ring, which is partly shaded by lots of greenery.

On special nights, the (hollow) white 'candles' can be made to light up, glowing with the tiny electric bulbs embedded inside; and if you've turned the lights of the bedroom out, it's a lovely nightlight with which to go to sleep. So gentle, so comforting.

Every few seconds the old-man Gnome 'speaks'—that is to say one large air bubble floats up from the gap between his conical magic cap and his fluted musical base column—and you can almost hear the fairies trill with happiness as they catch each and every word as it goes up and up, till finally it goes plop at the surface of the water, and sends expanding ripples in rhythmic sequence all over everyone's head.

Air bubble words of wisdom to which everyone listens, except the two sentries that is; the red one and the blue one, guarding the East and the West, and maintaining safe the whole magic circle. They're much too big and strong to hear old-man Gnome, and seem to pay no more attention to his bubble words than do ordinary grown-ups. Such a pity, really.

Often we and the fairies dance in the magic circle—notice how we've trodden the sand into ups and downs as we leap and frolic in and out of the white candles, in and around old-man Gnome and his bubbles and the expanding circles on the water sky. That is to say, everyone except the two sentries, who have to guard their posts, and except the grown-ups, of course, who miss all our fun.

Plants: 1 Cabomba, 2 Ambulia, 3 Hygrophila, 4 Myriophyllum. Rocks and other features: A English crystal, B plastic fluted base topped with Venetian crystal conical hat, C candle. *Note:* tank plan shows view from above.

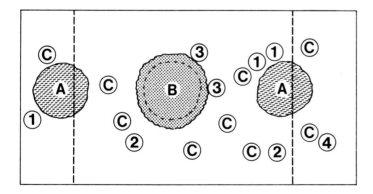

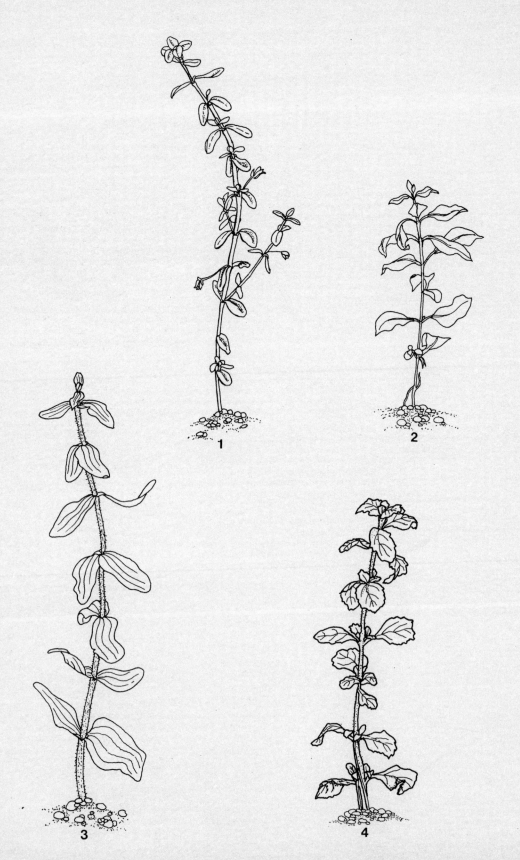

1

2

3

4

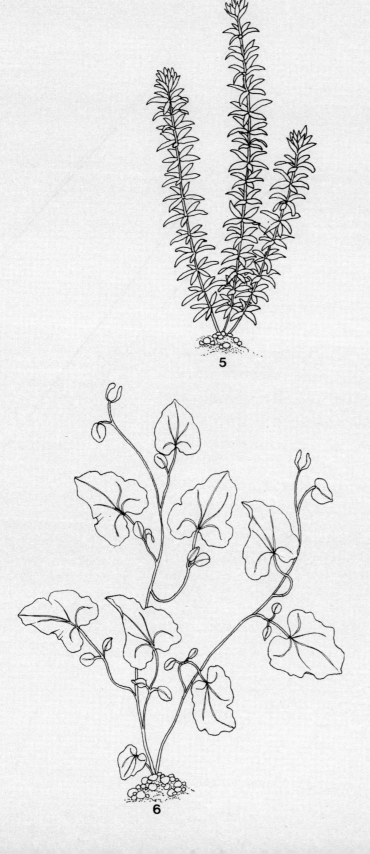

5

6

These all look best in clumps; they are available everywhere.

1
Bacopa monniera is standard favourite, with bright-green, slightly pulpy leaves and slightly hairy stem; similar varieties have more rounded leaves.

2
Ludwigia palustris has light-green leaves, and grows to some 18″; when hungry, sends down runners from nodes even from 6″ above soil; tolerates 55°F, but prefers about 70°.

3
Bacopa amplexicaulis can emerse, and grow to 30″, but is easily trimmed to tank size; hairy stem houses micro-organisms; plant turning dark green indicates something amiss.

4
Ludwigia natans is great sturdy-leaved favourite, with warm red tinge to underleaf: can emerse, but usually grows only to 6–8″ before lower leaves shed to produce stalky appearance.

5
Elodea densa is also known as *Anacharis densa*; has graced tanks and ponds for years; prefers 50-60°F, but is so hardy that it adapts to almost any conditions.

6
Cardamina lyrata is hardy, with bright green leaves; will tolerate 55-65°F; always hungry and sends out trailing shoots from main stem.

red indian sand picture

Painting pictures in the sand is a Red Indian art increasingly adapted for aquaria; we have added tree-bark to heighten the 'wigwam' effect which will be accentuated by the shadows thrown by overhead lighting; these shadows will also soften the glare of the highly coloured sand (compare the effect with that on page 34). The arrangement of the colours and the shape of the layout gives the illusion of a landscape retreating into a distant background, the horizon/skyline. Sparse plants are added to a vague openness of space, which is prevented from being bleak by the inherent gaiety of the colours.

Air bubbles add movement, especially as they crawl up the bark when released at the base; and secondly, pin-point shafts of lighting periodically replace the evenly diffused overhead lights shown opposite. We often use multi-phased lighting in our special tanks. A typical sequence would be: even diffusion; pause, when all is unlit; piercing shafts of pinpoint accuracy (carefully aimed at chosen targets); pause again, unlit; then a floor of coloured light (perhaps of more than one colour, eg red/blue/orange blend); and so on.

Our set-up has red strips in the foreground and blue vista in the rear; but many variations are open to you on these colour themes: the front strips can be broad, narrow, dotted or lace-worked; the rear can be single colour, multi-coloured, with or without shapes and smudges like clouds drifting in the distance. Add air bubbles in a stream, or in a curtain (a long diffuser of say 12″ with a line of bubbles escaping every ¼″) plus phased lighting as already suggested, and you'll never get your friends to take their eyes off it!

Plants: 1 Ambulia, 2 Ludwigia, 3 Vallisneria, 4 Cryptocoryne, 5 Bacopa. 'Rocks': all bark. *Note:* tank plan shows view from above.

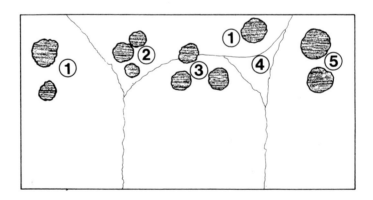

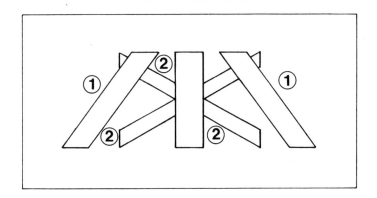

Plan for 'royal crown', pp. 78-9.
Plants: 1 Ivy leaf, 2 Hygrophila. Crown: made from acrylic sheeting cut into strips. *Note:* tank plan shows view from above.

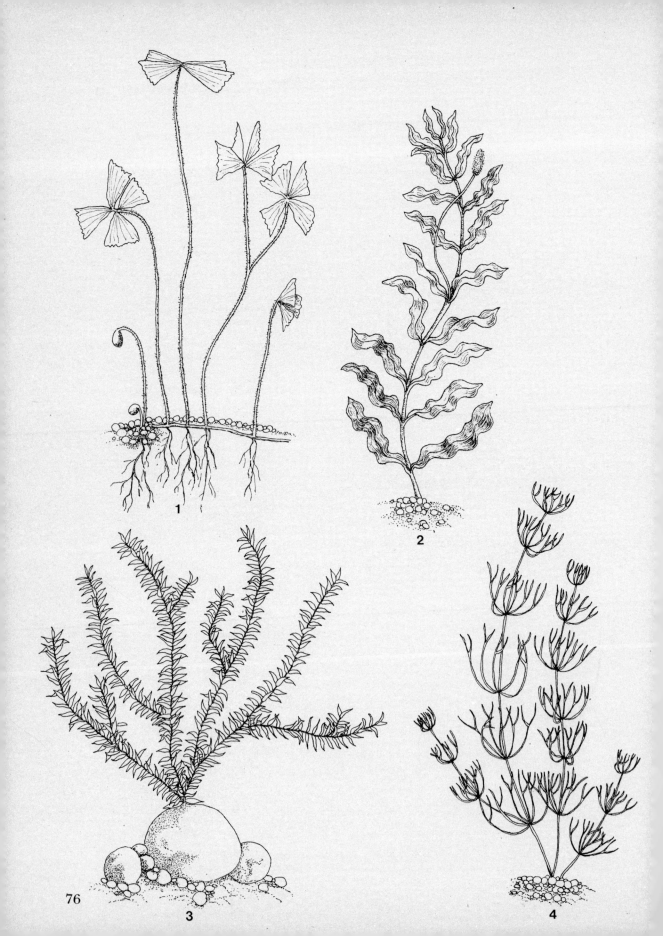

1

2

3

4

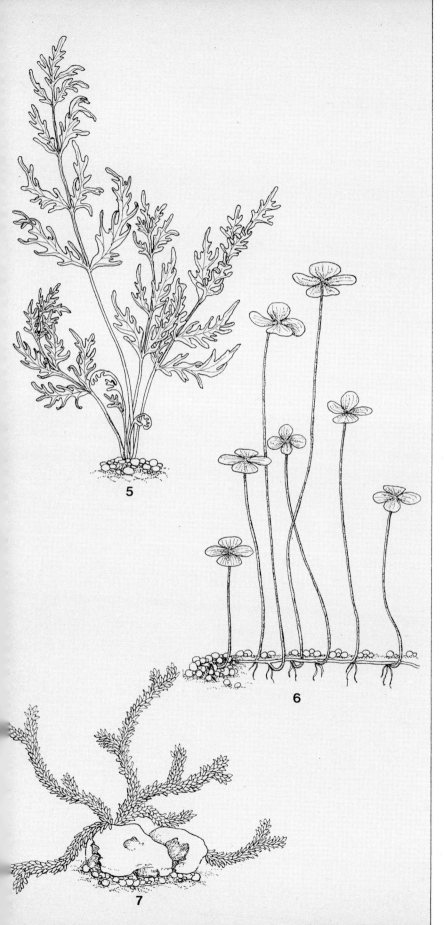

5

6

7

Unusual combinations of colour and type are possible (a base spreader like Marsilea should not be used with Nitella-like growths).

1
Marsilea hirsuta grows like tiny underwater forest to form swaying carpet some 4″ above soil level.
2
Potamogeton crispus is a clinger, lovely gold/red when mature; sways with any current and seeks new anchorages; tolerates almost any water.
3
Fontinalis antipyretica is tough, luxuriant, dark green; can anchor itself even on rocks; goes brown (usually) at the lower stems under strain; tolerates 45°F.
4
Nitella flexilis is very tenacious and spreads rapidly; tolerates almost any water, even brackish, and low temperatures.
5
Ceratopteris thalictroides is fast-growing, with light-green, fragile leaves; any old bit that breaks off can root; yellows if light is too strong, darkens if hungry.
6
Marsilea quadrifolia will carpet any area it can; upward growth from 3–30″ depending on conditions; tolerates dim light and 55°F.
7
Vesicularia dubyana grows branches of robust yellow-green that cling to anything; tends to grow out of tank.

royal crown

A more sophisticated sand-picture of European inspiration
which we planned for Queen Elizabeth II's Jubilee Year. Note
the finesse of the quadruple sand base striped lengthways in
four colours; the three national colours red/white/blue (found
in the flags of many nations including Britain, France and the
USA) are anchored on the yellow/gold of Truth and
symbolically representing 'the four corners of the earth' on
which the royal crown rests—visible to all, from all sides; there
is no back or front in this design which can go slap in the
middle of your room and be pleasant to view wherever you are.
To that end we have harmonized the green and white ivy leaves
at each extremity, holding the lovely red Hygrophila within.

We have used thin acrylic strips of plastic, which are
obtainable in many breath-taking colours—strong, pastel,
opaque, translucent, and phosphorescent.

The beauty of this striking yet simple design is that it makes

the tank look bigger than it is, as the sweeping curves of the crown and the thrusting peaks of the plants fill and swell the whole tank to give the maximum eye-catching effect. Notice how the plants in the centre practically break water as they tower up.

Enormously effective, too, is hidden and submerged lighting within the crown; this can be done by 'clearing a hole' in the tank's glass base, holding the sand back and then playing a light upwards through the base of the tank to flood the interior of the crown with light; or, if the tank is big enough, to bury a water-proof electric bulb (like the ones used in garden ponds) inside the sand within the crown. A final joy would be the addition of phased lighting alternating between different colours, and the streaming movement of air bubbles hugging the curves of the crown.

See tank plan and key, p. 75.

outdoor plants
and display

Almost any plant that grows naturally in your locality should be usable. There is certain to be a profusion of choice, and your specialist dealer may well have imported even more. Many of the 'indoor' plants already shown in the drawings will survive outdoors, and with the extra space will grow up handsomely above the water-surface. The dividing line between 'indoor' and 'outdoor' plants is not hard and fast.

Establishing a good balance between floating plants, submerged plants that do real (but unseen) work in keeping down the algae and in oxygenating the water, and the magnificent Lilies with the protective wide-spreading leaves and beautiful blooms, is a fairly obvious matter. For a 12'×6' pond you might need say three Lilies evenly spread, and six bunches of submerged plants, of twelve stems per bunch. This allows room for growth. The number of marginal, or bog, plants that grow round the edge is usually restricted by the soil area available.

But the balance between the plants as a whole and all the other factors like climate, trees, and soil is likely to be imposed by Mother Nature, and the gentle path of co-operation may yield the greatest beauty: of flowers, of foliage, of aquatic and air life, of harmony. Our photographs illustrate this. The plant life is of England, but is widely found in America and Asia, with local variations. Fish have not been prominently featured, and the photographs are of 'balances' that favour visible greenery, a delightful and restful vista of peace; which should be entirely practical for you to reproduce, formal or natural, flowing water or still pool, small and homely or great and expensive; all these possibilities are there for you to choose.

Plants at home in or beside water—Iris, Water Lilies (Nymphaea), and, in the background, a Willow tree.

81

lily pond

Still water—the edges are defined, the slope is gentle and therefore the owner has some control over the soil composition of the base.

Lilies have been given preference, and the underwater oxygenating plants have been pushed into the odd corners, so that Mother Nature has rectified the imbalance by encouraging floating plants and by stationing thrusting marginals like Iris and Rushes right inside the water.

Small aquatic life like snails and water-boatmen would adapt; fish would tend to wilt; but external life would flourish and the air would hum with insect life.

The great advantage is ease of maintenance—algae have been inhibited because the Lilies have asserted themselves and have consumed the micro-foods. Man need do little more than leave well alone, provided the pond is big enough.

If this balance were attempted in a plastic-lined miniature then the labour of cleaning would be immense, and the stagnation and decay would be noticeable. But as shown, this is a set-up ideal for temperate and changeable climates where mosquitos don't bother you too much, and where rain is frequently washing clean, part-changing the water, damping down the insects, and reviving the wilting fish.

Strictly aquatic marginal plants have also largely been displaced: the stone-rimmed peninsula houses garden plants; and most effective they look too—a squat, clumpy foil for the glorious spread of the Lilies.

An ornamental pond with naturalized plantings of Zebra Rush, Iris, and Astilbe, with Water Lilies.

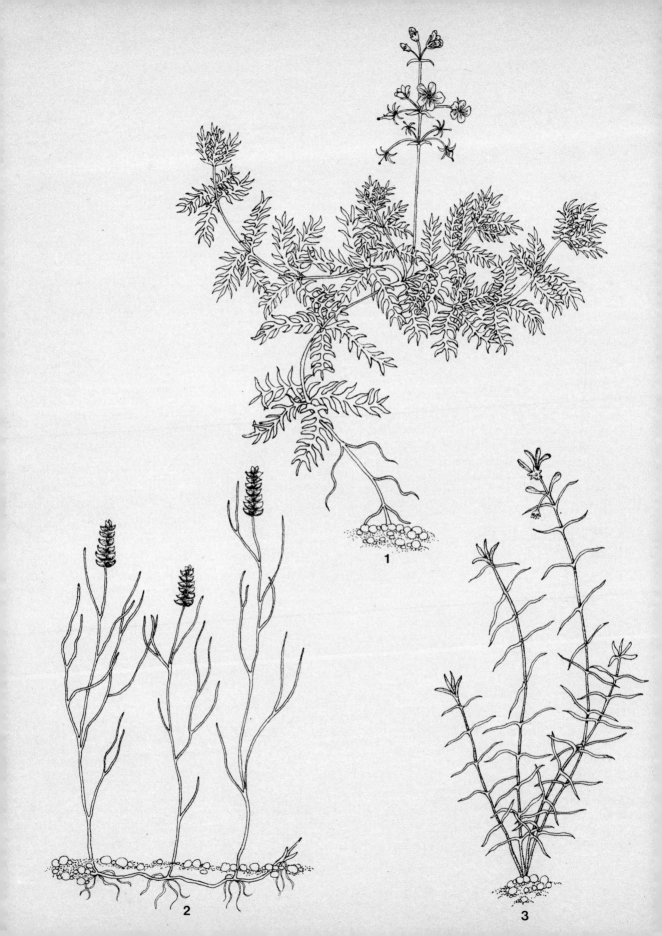

1

2

3

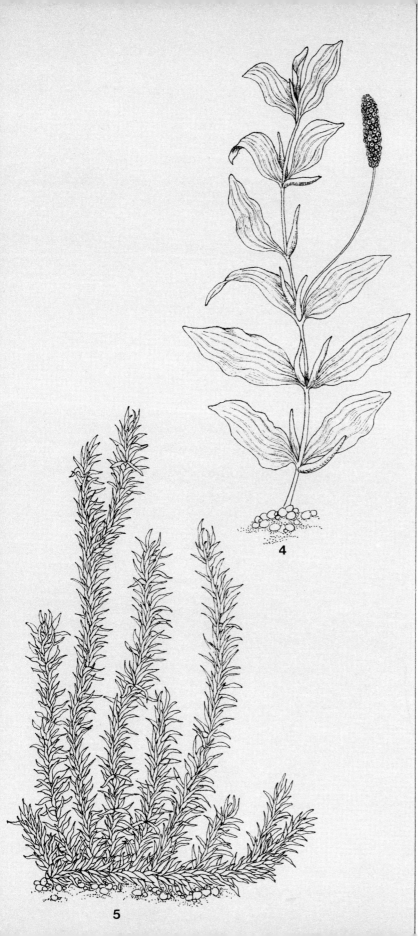

4

5

These are tolerant of cold, tough and popular; a contrast of types is shown, but one wide-spreading plant per pond is usually enough.

1
Hottonia palustris tolerates cold; sporadic sunshine gives red tinges to bright green floating leaves; produces beautiful, violet, emersed flowers.

2
Potamogeton filiformis is tough with leaf quite different from *P. lucens*—yellow-green, with yellow-brown cone flower; thrusts towards light, and sends runners everywhere.

3
Crassula aquatica is rather small, growing to only 10″; prefers cold, though warmth darkens yellow-green stems and 'needle' leaves.

4
Potamogeton lucens has strong, bright-green, surface-floating leaves, and green 'cone' flower; Typical of many varieties of this genus, though some show brown and red tinges.

5
Lycopodium inundatum is green and lush and tolerates cold; emits unpleasant smell in certain seasons/conditions, especially if water pH is below 6.0.

goldfish pond

The good old oldie, the round pond; in this case the fountain is at the side.

This set-up could as easily be an instant already-moulded plastic pond, a plastic-lined pond, or a cement pond; it can be of almost any size, but seldom more than 1'–1' 6" deep. The stone capping round the rim could be large chippings or great big flag-stones.

Haphazard is the plant growth inside, with the balance easily altered with changes of climate; being shallow the water soon reflects the external fluctuations of sun/cloud or frost and the poor plant life does not really know what to do. Higher life-forms like delicate Lilies would give up, hardy annuals would survive although perhaps not flourish; the quick-spurting algae would proliferate at each burst of sunshine but could soon run out of food in the restricted conditions of soil/water depth; our photograph shows the current truce between emergent rush and struggling Lily bloom.

Enthusiastic owners can have a great time trying to modify Mother Nature:

(1) Add fertilizers, plant in pots, and flower your chosen plants, eg Lilies. Support with floating electric heaters.

(2) Add filters, keep the water sweet, and encourage your fish.

(3) Add lights and let your fountain spray, and have lovely sounds of falling waters thrilling with splashing colours. Most, most refreshing in hot climates; and expansive in restricted space. It can suit everyone's pocket, and taste.

The goldfish in this pond are at home with growths, as yet undeveloped, of Iris, Sweet Flag, Water Lilies, and Water Hyacinth.

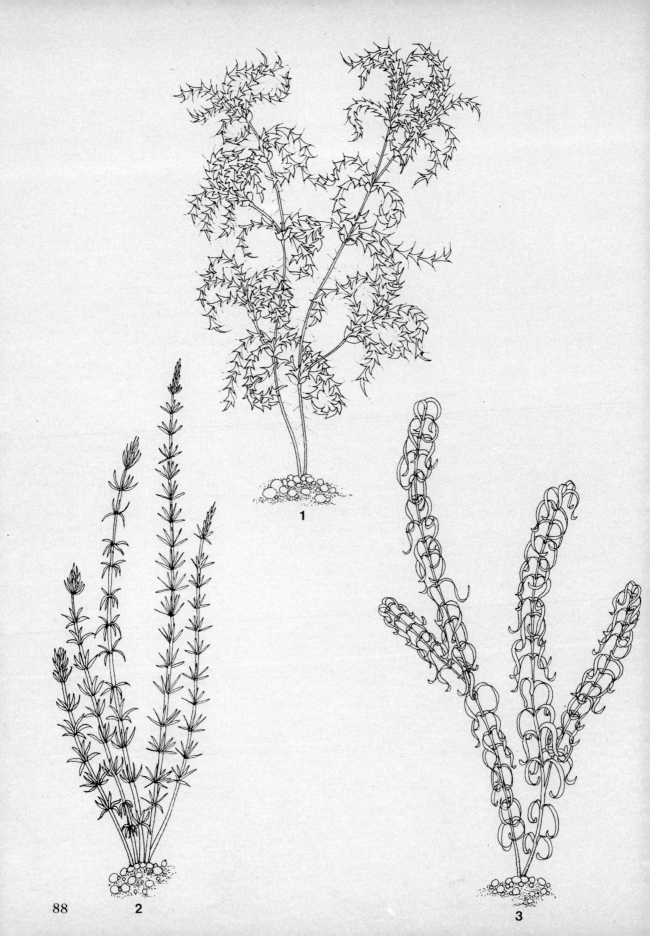

88 2 1 3

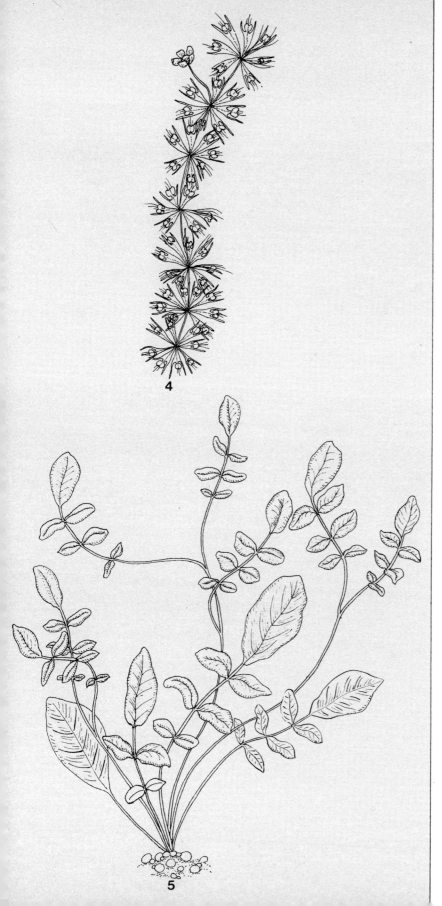

4

5

Here is a mixture of the known and the unusual; all are vigorous, striking and useful.

1
Nagas minor survives cold, mulm or stagnation, although delicate leaves break early; bottle-green at growth nodes, shading to bright green; hairy stems.
2
Hippuris vulgaris is popular, prolific, and emerses readily; some stems 20″ long and richly tufted.
3
Elodea canadensis is widely known, often as *Anacharis canadensis*; there are many sub-species—shown is heavily curled, lush-green variety inhibited only by temperature above 70°F.
4
Aldrovandia vesiculosa can float if rooting is difficult; carnivorous—traps prey in bristles or leaf glands; useful for removing unwanted water-pests.
5
Rorippa amphibia is curious in that top floaters are tiny compared to vigorous underwater growth; fast-growing and widely available.

on a grand scale

This is a magnificent 'pond', a small lake, which can be designed easily so as to be sweetened by a running, natural stream.

The soil goes right down to the edge, and then has dribbled into the water to cover the whole base, allowing a mass of submerged plants to carpet and to overwhelm all others—no Lilies, no floating plants, just a few tough Iris that thrive in such soil anyway.

The main emphasis is then: firstly sweet (and flowing) water; secondly the surrounding marginals reaching to a profusion of thick clumps, tall and with flowers—healthy, expansive greenery challenging the very garden itself. The pond side has been dominated and outshone. The fish are just scavengers here, eating mosquito larvae.

Curiously enough, you could reproduce this approach in miniature with an elongated pond covered by an inexpensive pond lining, adding recirculating water to give the essential water flow (perhaps even playing it over a small waterfall), provided your soil and climate suit such green growth. In miniature, your reliance on fertilizers would need to supplement your lack of soil volume, and part-changes of water might prevent possible sourness and festering. Abutting right onto, even into, a small lawn, the total effect could be gorgeous. Obviously you would screen all artificial items; for example, the rim of the pond lining would actually be buried by adjoining soil in which plants will have rooted, maintaining the illusion of a natural stream trickling up from below ground. Irregular edging and slight sloping should be encouraged.

In the foreground and along the left bank, *Primula florindae, P. helodoxa,* and *P. japonica*; with the broad leaves, *Hosta undulata*; and in the right foreground, *Iris pallida variegata.*

1

2

3

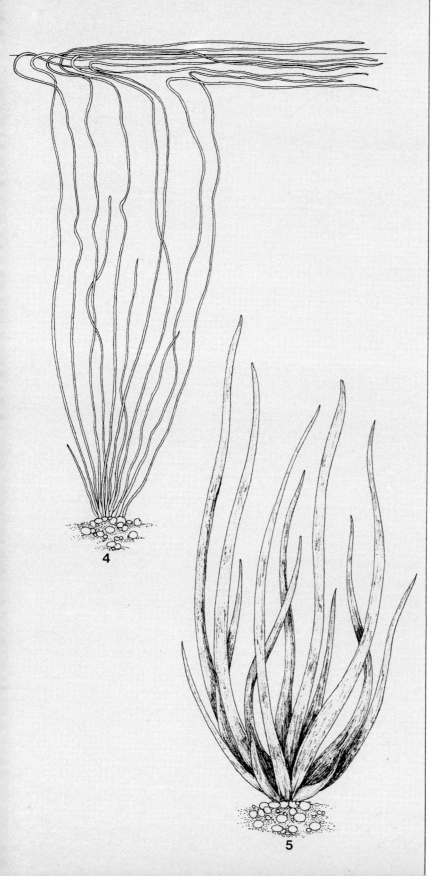

Five strong growers,
capable of expanding.

1

Elisma natans is affected in
its leaf shape by
conditions, and when it
emerses; bottle-green
leaves and yellow-white
flowers with brown centres
typical, but variations
common.

2

Subularis aquatica is similar
to grassy Sagittarias, with
large, triangular emersed
leaves; yellow/white grow
sparsely round spike;
prefers cold water.

3

Lobelia dortmanna is widely
popular; too-dark green
leaves indicate strain;
produces delicate sky-blue
flowers; prefers cold and
poor soils, even sand.

4

Isoetes malinvernia has
tremendous surface-
trailing extrusions, often
twisted in a spiral; yellow
tinged with green.

5

Isoetes lacustris tolerates
cold and grows in chalk,
peat—even sand; vigorous
dark, bottle-green leaves
usually restricted by
conditions to 8″, but can
grow to 20″.

lilies

Such gorgeous blooms, such lovely colours, such alluring shapes—there are over 200 varieties of Lily available, with new ones frequently added. Everyone loves them, and all tastes are catered for in their incredible range. Here we show two very fine examples.

Lysichitum americanum is noted for its emersed blooms, standing-proud and high above the water—welcoming and protective cups framing the inner inflorescence, starkly contrasting with the cones and spikes of contrasting yellow/green.

The James Brydon Water Lily is a much-loved example of the Lily's trailing leaf and floating bloom, with its superb buds and flowers. The leaves can have a very wide span, and all manner of wild life, from frogs to birds, will alight on them; it really is delightful to see sparrows pecking and pruning them, and even bathing on/from them. So, too, will fish such as sticklebacks snuggle up/under them.

Leaf colouring varies with the conditions, and our illustrations show some of the range. Yellow tinges or heavy curling can be an early pointer to stagnation below; when sheeny greens glow, this can suggest vigorous growth below.

Top: *Lysichitum americanum.*

Bottom: *Nymphaea* 'James Brydon'.

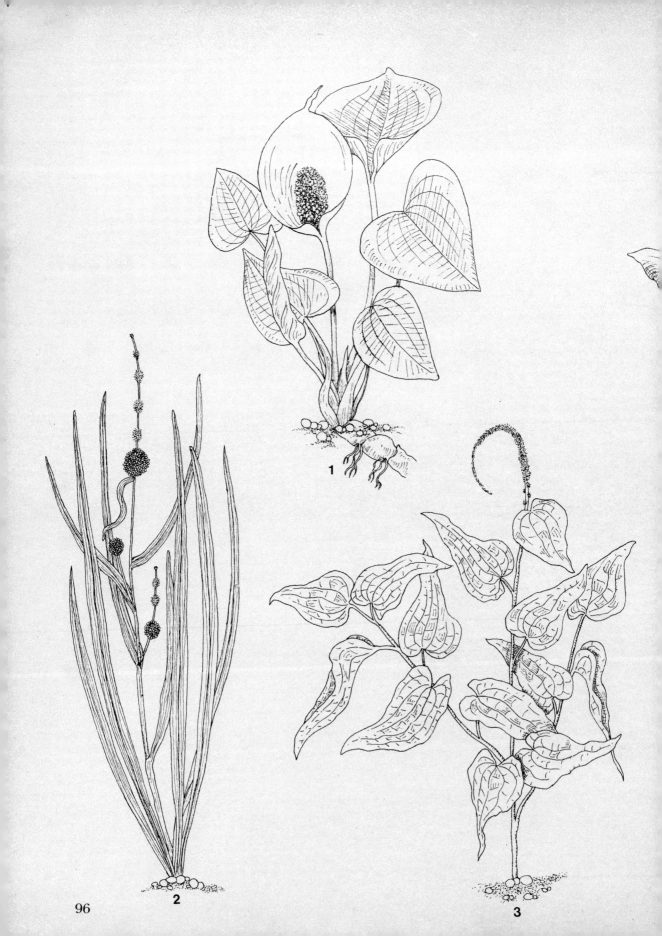

1

2

3

4

5

Some contrasts in growing habit—allow enough room for these.

1

Calla palustris has yellow and dark-brown two-tone leaves; flower colouring the reverse of leaves, centre darker and flecked with yellow/green; white tinges prominent in some conditions.

2

Sparganium erectum is another very aggressive tall thruster from runners; produces vertically striped green leaves, with green and fawn flower spikes.

3

Saururus cernuus thrusts up from fast-spreading runners to produce luxuriant yellow-green leaves with unstable white and yellow flower spikes, flopping over in crook shape; dominates and overpowers if unchecked.

4

Ceratopteris thalictroides is pond version of *Trapa natans;* can float or root, according to conditions; core of plant yellow, shading to green—yellow encroaches as water becomes less favourable.

5

Sparganium americanum is American counterpart of *S. erectum,* similar in colouring, but with accentuated flower spikes; produces yellow rather than green leaves if atmospheric warmth too low.

patio pool

Easy to build at home with a plastic liner, with a prefabricated plastic unit, or with the conventional concrete—your patio pond can be as big or as deep as conditions warrant, and can abut onto grass or have a formal trim: our illustration shows both. Note the 'natural'-looking protective wall of 'stones' on the grass side to discourage excess soil from washing into the pond with the rain, and on the house side to guard against the entry of picnic débris and the like.

Shallow-water bog plants growing out nicely merge into the surroundings and can flower in season; central Lilies in profusion, with a few submerged oxygenating plants, all combine to give a stable balance.

There are two snags to this otherwise deservedly popular set-up: firstly, in temperate zones where sun and rain alternate, the quicker-spurting algae, as we have seen, can be a nuisance (the site is fully exposed to intermittent sun)—shading with garden umbrellas, or with wood or wicker fencing, etc, are both preferable to the falling leaves of an over-shadowing tree. Secondly, unless there is a distinct drop at the bottom of the garden, you will not be able to siphon off water to clean/clear the pond of algae. An electric pump will save a lot of work, as well as providing a pleasing and helpful fountain, and our illustration shows this working nicely.

We suggest that you plant in pots, rather than introduce all-over sand on the pond base, to facilitate maintenance.

Water Lilies, Iris, and Primula are the plantings in this more formal approach.

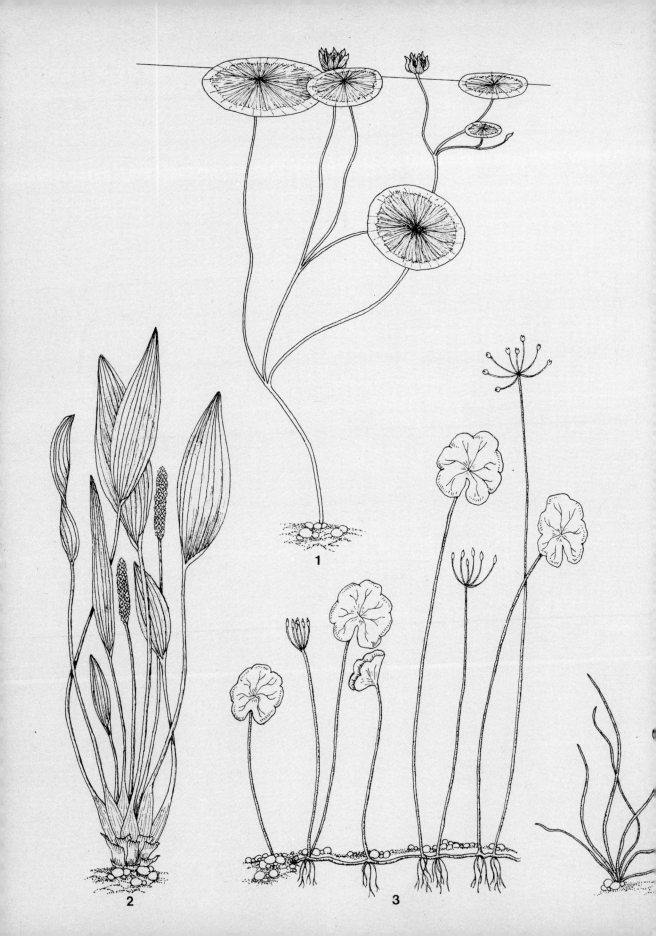

1

2

3

4

5

6

All these deserve to be better known than they are; hardy, they are fairly widely available, and expand well if soil is rich enough.

1

Brasenia schreberi is another spreader from USA, with bright-red stems and vivid yellow/green two-toned leaves rimmed with red (whole leaf reddens at fruition); purple-red flower encloses a mustard-coloured centre.

2

Orontium aquaticum grows vigorously with yellow-green leaves (blue-green when specially happy) and profuse yellow cone-shaped flowers.

3

Hydrocotyle vulgaris has hairy, yellow-gold stems supporting surface-floating leaves, dark-green with white veins; flowers emerse, white and gold in colour.

4

Alisma plantago is light-green favourite emersing readily and producing fine inflorescence waving in wind; excess leaf curl signals distress.

5

Sagittaria latifolia changes leaf shape according to conditions and on emersing; the stronger the green the happier the plant; flowers have white petals, red trim and yellow centre.

6

Echinodorus tenellus is fast spreader native to USA; runners grope anywhere they might root.

101

hydroponics

by Philippa Katz

Nature has contrived to adapt herself and exploit our planet in so many extraordinary ways that despite, or because of, modern scientific knowledge, the world of plant growth is a constant source of wonder and astonishment. This fascination has led to unprecedented interest in all aspects of plant behaviour or adaptation—leaves drooping when water is scarce, flower heads turning towards the sun, even the texture of leaves, thick and shiny evergreens in the rain forest where too much water must always be repelled to prevent rotting, and with grey felt-like outer layers in the desert to protect against fierce sun.

From interest has come the emphasis on care—if we relax delightedly in an atmosphere of vigorous green life, then we must learn how to observe and respond to the needs of the plants. Air, light and warmth are fairly easy to provide, and garden shops label our new plants with their requirements. But we must add water and nourishment. With ordinary soil-growing pots this may not be so simple, and the more we understand, the more complex the problem becomes. Poor soil with bad drainage, soil too acid or too alkaline, too sandy or too heavy—the difficulties often seem endless.

We have also begun to appreciate the ways in which soil pests and soil-borne disease can destroy everything from tiny seedlings to full-grown trees. Even the beginner therefore soon learns that absolutely sterile soil or a soilless growing medium give the best chance of germination and healthy growth for every kind of seed.

It is gardening without soil that this part of the book is about.

Why has soilless gardening taken so long to reach our living-rooms? We see in the nursery catalogues and lists that plants live in all sorts of habitats where soil may not be present, but that every known plant needs some source of water some time in its life. The image of soil has persisted, however, as the source of life, Mother Earth as the cradle for our children, the nourisher of our bodies, and the symbol of everything good and wholesome—and until recently water-gardening other than in tanks or ponds has been restricted to the commercial area, apparently too exact a science to be of interest to anyone except technicians and too artificial a process to be adaptable to the relaxed domestic environment.

The very popularity of the back-to-Nature movement has brought the fields and streams of the countryside into the cities and towns. We want and we need growing plants around us: green spikes that reach to the ceiling; green feathers that flow gently in the breeze from an open window; scented flowers that fill a room with fragrance in the middle of winter; herbs and vegetables to pick from the branch when ripe and heavy with flavour. In short, we want the best of yesterday living in the midst of tomorrow. With this desire to enrich our surroundings has come the realisation that there exists a simple, clean system of soilless gardening, a system which gives us the pleasures of real gardening in an almost fool-proof modern form, convenient and involving no great efforts of care and maintenance.

This system is hydroponics, which is beginning to come down from the ivory tower and into our everyday lives. The 'dictionary' definition of hydroponics (*hudor*, water; *ponos*, working; both from the Greek) is 'the science of growing plants in a nutrient solution instead of soil'. Many modern books call it 'soilless gardening', 'indoor water gardening', or even, as a compromise, 'hydro-culture'.

What follows is not a comprehensive guide, but an introduction to a new and fascinating hobby. We hope it will lead you to go into the subject in greater depth, and join the growing number of hydroponicists all over the world.

why hydroponics? the pros and cons
As children, many of us have put an avocado stone in a glass jar, with the water just covering the bottom of the stone, and watched the roots develop below and the green stems grow above. As long ago as the 1880s domestic books were describing 'hyacinth jars' which held the bulb on a special rim just above the surface of the water—a simple and effective way of bringing spring fragrance and colour into chilly rooms in wintertime.

This is the simplest introduction to hydroponics—not only for avocados and bulbs; almost any plant can be grown in water, as long as we add nutrients to the liquid, ensuring long-term health and vigour.

The advantages are many.

At one stroke we do away with the two main causes of failure for the amateur plant-lover—faulty watering and soil-borne pests and diseases. Lack of water is one common hazard of conventional gardening, unless you are around your plants for a good part of the day. During the summer, sudden changes in temperature are quite common, as the early morning coolness suddenly becomes a scorching afternoon. Even a few hours in an unventilated room with sunlight intensified by window glare can check a growing plant tip so drastically that it never recovers its vigour. Winter brings the dry heat of radiators during the day to desiccate plant cells plus an abrupt drop at night as the heating is turned off. A missed morning or two, an unexpected absence for three or four days, and the returning traveller may well find a roomful of dried-out sticks instead of the luxuriant green foliage left behind.

Even for plan-ahead vacations, anyone who has more than one or two plants knows that quite a lot of preparation is

Growing a plant from an avocado pip in a jar. The pip is held by four matchsticks stuck into the side, which rest on the rim of the jar.

involved, with various contraptions of water tanks or individual plastic wraps plus, if possible, a kind neighbourly plant-sitter to check on day-to-day condition.

Over-watering is the other side of the coin. Dry-as-dust soil is self-evidently a problem, but few plant owners realise that constant over-watering can make the soil so soggy and clogged that fine root hairs literally drown in mud. Pouring water on an already saturated plant is surprisingly common, since the top layer of soil may dry out while the roots are still soaking wet, and they will rot away unseen until quite suddenly the plant collapses. Watering the right amount at the right time can be a real art, and unless you become attuned to the subtle needs of each plant, it can be a very time-consuming and hit-or-miss affair.

Soil is the second area of hazard. In the city, just finding good soil can be an enormous problem. There are many ready-mixed composts for various purposes, it's true, but these are quite expensive, and as you become more adventurous and knowledgeable with new and different kinds of plants, you will find that each individual pot needs a slightly different mix. If you buy the compost components in bulk, they must be stored in a cool dry place, and wetted thoroughly before potting up. Even with specialist mixtures, growing plants will need repotting quite often, as soil must be renewed as the nutrients are exhausted or removed by watering. The scattering of earth and manure on sink and floor seems to have a magical yen for your finest carpets and curtains. Newspaper spread out on tables never manages to catch all the dirt, and creepy-crawlies find their way out of the plants into our furniture, or hibernate in one pot and then find their way to all the others during re-potting time or when the spring comes. If you use garden soil it may carry all kinds of virus and infectious diseases, aside from common pests, which may not survive the rigours of outdoor life and the activities of voracious birds, but will flourish indoors and multiply as never before.

When using soil at all we make the plants work hard for their food. The various elements required for growth are locked into the particles of earth, and must be dissolved and converted before the plant roots will take them up. And we are still discovering tiny quantities of minerals which must be present for the best results—nature is full of complex interacting organisms and constituents, and if one or two are missing then the whole system may break down. Strange deficiencies such as the lack of boron or copper may result in poor growth or scorched leaves, and even the expert can easily be baffled.

One of the advantages of hydroponics, on the other hand, is that by making up a solution according to a given formula, or, even more simply, using a ready-prepared powder, we make sure that every known requirement is taken care of in a liquid form which the plant can absorb immediately. The result is quicker and healthier growth.

Growing your plants in water will not only add to your chances of 'green-fingered' success with a minimum of care, but will give you two important plusses—the decorative and visual pleasure of twining root systems in glass containers, and the fun of beginning an exciting and rewarding hobby which offers untold possibilities for ornamental and useful greenery everywhere.

the history of hydroponics

Hydroponics sprang from the enormous thirst for knowledge and interest in experimentation which swept over the western world at the end of the 18th century. Until then, the different theories of how plants grew were based on two ancient beliefs. There were those who felt that water was the sole source of life and nourishment, and others who felt equally sure that earth alone was capable of supporting life. As the new sciences grew and developed, the great explorers and plant-hunters dis-

More basic hydroponics! Growing Ivy in a milk bottle—the 'solution' method requires no aggregate to support the plant, provided a suitable container is used.

covered and classified new species under the influence of Linnaeus and Darwin, and their notes, drawings and speculations changed the course of botanical science all over the world.

At the same time Bourssault and Kleber began their work on how many plants, whatever their species, managed to stay alive in a sometimes hostile atmosphere. The advance of chemistry meant that matter could be separated more scientifically into components. Experimenting with solutions containing various salts and minerals, investigators proved conclusively that growth and development took place with plants bedded in sand, quartz, charcoal—or indeed any solid granular matter which acted as support for the root system and stem—as long as the correct nutrition was supplied in liquid form. This system was perfect for laboratory work; each kind of plant food could be isolated and fed to individual plants and the effect noted. Over the years, accumulated notes taught the scientists what formulae would give good results, and by the 1920s different research centres all over the world had favourite 'recipes'.

The two main techniques still in use today were standardized at an early stage. One (our old friend the avocado stone) relies on the stem being supported by a jar or wire mesh, or even a layer of sterile wadding, with the root system growing freely in a trough or bowl of nutrient solution. This was particularly useful when root development was being studied, and it remains a delightful, often decorative method for home gardeners, with the roots forming strange and complex patterns in the liquid. However, with larger plants it can cause problems as the weight of the top growth is difficult to balance on the support. Another drawback is the need to change the solution fairly frequently, as otherwise salts and minerals may accumulate in the stagnant liquid.

The second system involved bedding the plants in some sort of sterile granular material as a means of support, usually called the aggregate, and diluting the nutrient in a watering-can and adding it to the aggregate when required or according to a prepared timetable.

During the early part of this century soilless plant-growing remained the interest of the scientific community only, a convenient way of studying growth patterns and nutritional requirements without the unpredictable onslaughts of poor weather conditions, climatic changes, pests and other 'natural' problems. 'Real' gardeners and commercial producers dug and manured their soil, planted their crops, watched the skies anxiously, and relied on another kind of expert who built new machinery and bred disease-resistent and high-yielding strains of grains and vegetables.

Pioneering is not always easy, particularly in a field as traditional and conservative as horticulture, but one Dr William F. Gericke, of the University of California, was so successful in his efforts that his plants out-grew and out-produced every comparable variety of food and flower crop. The publication of his trials results in the 1930s started a flood of hydroponics research stations everywhere.

Commercial firms began to take a close interest in mass-production, building sheds and greenhouses on sites unsuitable for ordinary horticulture. With careful control, acres of tomatoes and carnations grew, growing luxuriantly on desert sands in the Middle East and on hard-clay in Russia. Almost all countries from Scandinavia to the Seychelles now have some sort of hydroponics centre, and the future industrial possibilities are even more exciting.

For the plant-lover, anxious to have a potful of greenery growing happily and healthily in every room, hydroponics has really come of age. Now, with all the experience and knowledge culled from hundreds of thousands of amateur growers in every country, we know that hydroponics can be easily adapted to home conditions. The basic nutritional formulae are available in powder or tablet form, and containers can be adapted or bought in almost every garden shop of any size.

Far from being a complicated technical device, hydroponic culture is the simplest and most convenient way of making your own particular bit of desert bloom—and keep on blooming—in winter, summer, vacation-times or holidays. We've shown you earlier in the book how plants can grow under the water or on top of the water, in a self-sufficient environment where fish and plants create their own natural habitat (with a little help from you!). Here now is another kind of water-gardening, where a few simple rules will lead you to a creative and satisfying hobby capable of producing food for your table and beauty for your mind all the year round.

how you begin
The easiest way to understand the few simple rules of water culture is to begin with what a plant needs to grow: water, of course; light for the photosynthesis process; air; and nourishment in the form of various mineral salts which when dissolved in water are absorbed through the roots and

Left: The aggregate system. With some containers, water is drawn up into the aggregate from a separate reservoir, for example by means of a wick, or by capillary attraction; with others, such as the very simple arrangement shown here, water and nutrient is poured into the pot—the plug at the bottom enables it to be drained off for periodic renewal and for aeration of the roots and aggregate.

Right: The suspension system in its simplest and perhaps most traditional form—the Hyacinth jar.

circulated throughout the plant system. These are the life-giving ingredients for all plant forms in varying degrees. The final requirement is a purely physical one—since plants have no bone tissue, they must have some base structure to support the leaves and stems. Many of the plants described earlier in the book use the water as a support—but most plants lock into some kind of firm support, where they can spread out the fine root-threads widely enough to stabilize the top growth and help the quick absorption of food.

With these basic necessities of life in mind, we can look at the two methods previously mentioned which are both useful in hydroponic gardening. In all cases, the solution should be changed once a week or every ten days.

Above, on the right, a plant is shown growing directly in solution. The plant is suspended over the water-plus-nutrients, with the roots growing freely into the liquid. The special Victorian hyacinth jars hold the bulb firmly; without this supporting shelf, netting or a perforated tray is necessary, and for larger plants there will have to be a layer of gravel or small stones on top of the mesh to give additional stability.

There are many variations on suspended systems, for different types of plants and for different conditions. With all of them some sort of drainage plug is useful for quick emptying.

The other house-plant method, the more common of the two, uses a solid aggregate, a sterile, granular mixture, to support the plant much as the soil does. Incidentally, any support medium is usually called 'aggregate' in hydroponics, whether made from stone, glass, sand, plastic, rock or brick. The arrangement often looks exactly like an ordinary pot plant, with a pebble mulch on top of the earth! Almost any container can be adapted to this method—bowls, troughs, window-boxes, even kitchen sinks. The roots spread out and grow naturally into the spaces between the aggregate granules. The nutrient solution is poured into the container and percolates gently down, collecting at the bottom to act as a reservoir of water and food to be absorbed gradually upwards into the plant.

In fact, the two methods are really no more than different ways of supporting the plant; some plants lend themselves to suspension, particularly the smaller plants and bulbs, while others seem to fit more naturally into an aggregate base. Or you can combine the two, growing your plant in a clear glass container so you can see the root patterns, but providing clear glass chips or fragments to give them something to cling to and provide a little extra stability; this is particularly effective in a tall glass phial which could otherwise become top-heavy.

Now for the practical part: what equipment do you need for success? Luckily it is minimal and most of the requirements are inexpensive or adaptable and long-lasting.

containers

Almost any kind of container that holds 6-8″ of water will do, especially for smaller plants or decorative use on the dining-room table or a low coffee-table in the living-room. Glass, porcelain, aluminium, plastic—you name it, you can use it. Bottle-cutters will provide you with dozens of shapes from throw-away jars and jugs with cracked lips (but make sure that the crack doesn't extend into your new container!). Clear, amber, green or blue glass are all appropriate—the only difficulty with clear glass comes when it is left in strong or direct sunlight: algae will grow happily and very quickly, and the lovely pattern of twining, twisting roots will soon be obscured by a dirty-green film. One answer is to keep the pot covered during the day by a scarf or piece of thick paper wrapped around the container. But I find that since one of the advantages of hydroculture is the simple way a plant can be popped into a new container without any of the mess and trouble involved in re-potting, I usually keep my plants in dark containers, then for special occasions, transfer them to show off the 'string art' base. Ferns and other types which prefer shady spots can be grown in clear glass with almost no trouble except for a weekly scrub of the container when you drain and replace the liquid. Experiment and see—certainly the unearthly effect of a bowl full of growth below and a lacy green cascade above is worth an extra few minutes a week.

Ordinary flower pots can be adapted easily, with extra-deep saucers to make sure the nutrients don't drain off entirely. Clay or unglazed pottery is more absorbent than china or glass, and helps the nutrients travel up to the stem. Copper or brass always looks exciting with the varied tones of greenery, but these, as well as pewter or lead containers of any kind, will have to be lined with heavy plastic. Otherwise the water and the nutrient will react with the metal (as happens in cooking with old copper pans) and the plants may be poisoned or stunted. This is true even if the metal has been given a coat of supposedly water-proof lacquer; the lacquer is only a thin film, easily damaged by scratches or even dampness, so don't take a chance.

There are plenty of pots specially designed for the aggregate method. The simplest is a container with a drainage plug at the bottom; others consist of a pot with a conventional drainage hole placed in a deep saucer of water. The most modern are special double-walled pots, the inner bottom being of per-forated material—the solution is poured in to the correct level, and the roots draw the moisture and nourishment upwards as needed. Built-in drainage plugs, in whatever kind of container, are particularly useful for a number of plants growing together, or in large, low-standing displays such as a big trough in a bay window, or a heavy circular tub with a ten-foot palm. These are difficult to move around or lift up to drain off the liquid. Weight may be important, especially in apartments; adapt a plastic window-box in a simple modern style, or a not-too-dazzling reproduction in wrought iron or lead. The base of the unit should be far enough above the floor to let you slip a pan under the plug once a week while it drains, so make a pair of supports as high as a kitchen bowl. Simple wooden blocks are best—they can be painted or stained to match the box. Remember to mount the back of the container slightly higher than the front, so the tilt will let all the solution drain out. You'll also get a better view of your plants!

inside your container
With the solution method, of course, the container is filled with

liquid and the only feature you need inside it is a shelf just above the water level to hold the plant upright. In the garden, a simple wire mesh can be folded around the lip of the container to act as a support, but in the house or conservatory it is much better to fold the mesh inside or make a kind of interior table. A thin layer of gravel chips will hide the mesh if you find it too ugly or obtrusive.

The aggregate system offers a great many more possibilities. Remember that the aggregate particles must be large enough to allow air to move within the spaces. This is particularly true in dampish climates, where very find sand, as used in some early hydroculture experiments, may clog up the hairs and prevent the air reaching the root growth. Very large stones may be too heavy for the pot and damage the stem. Otherwise, the choice is remarkably wide. Your local hydroculture research station has information on the best inexpensive materials in your district, but in general you are safe with any small pebble or gravel mixture. The simplest source of aggregate may be very near at hand, for example well-washed cinders from coal fires or the coarser river sand, especially mixed with fine gravel or pebbles or peat moss. Aquarium gravel comes in beautiful colours, as we have shown earlier in the book—why not match the container to a toning gravel, or use marbles or glass chips, available in most craft shops? Where weight is important, especially if the container itself is heavy, use one of the newer plastic or ore-deposit products that are now widely distributed for mixing with ordinary composts—vermiculite is one, perlite another. Leca is a concrete-manufacturing product sometimes easily available and very cheap, especially if you live near a concrete factory. Slate shards, small bits of broken tiles or bricks, marble chips—explore your local shops. Anything smallish and easily cleaned and sterilized can be tried.

Finally, the solution. It doesn't seem to matter if your tap water is hard or soft. A simple testing kit will give you the acid/alkaline balance (the pH) of your water, and instructions on how to correct it if absolutely necessary. But few plants are really that sensitive. Chlorine is probably the most common additive and highly chlorinated water may make some plants unhappy. However, water left to stand for a day or two will lose most of its chlorine. Fill a gallon jug or a large bucket a day or two before your weekly feed, and keep it filled in between just in case you have an emergency. Try not to take water from a softener—it's nice to wash your hair in, but contains other chemicals to counteract the natural minerals, and the fewer

unwanted additives that go on your plants the better.

The nutrition you add is a different matter. For the beginner, buy one of the powders or tablets made up commercially for use in hydroponics; they are widely distributed, easy to use and almost infallible. If you mix them as directed you should have no problems. You will need a measuring spoon and a measuring jug. As you become more experienced, you may want to make up your own formulae, experiment with various different compounds, and watch how different plants are affected. Suppliers of chemical and fertilizer salts will usually be happy to send as much information as the customer can take—make sure they know you are interested in home hydroponics and not farming, or you may get huge catalogues of tractor-spray mixtures and weed-control products! Once you have reached this experimental stage, you are well on your way to being an expert hydroponicist!

A simple wick system involves a combination of the water and aggregate method. A double container is used. The base is filled with solution, leaving a gap of about ½″ for air. The inside container has a perforated base, about one hole every 4 square feet.

A thick wick is moistened and pulled through the holes, leaving two or three inches in the solution. Add a little aggregate, spread out the top of the wicks and add more aggregate. Leave until the moisture is drawn up and the aggregate is just damp.

Check the level of nutrient solution regularly, adding when necessary. Fresh solution should be used every week and the

Hydroculture containers designed and sold for the purpose. The right-hand illustration shows (left to right), Anthurium, Dracaena and Scindapsus; that on the left Philodendron and Neanthe.

VG—H

container can simply be tipped out, washed, refilled and the top replaced without disturbing the plants at all.

This method is extremely useful for smallish plants (not enough liquid is taken up for the gross feeders or large flowering plants) and especially for seeds.

A wick system—nutrient is drawn up the wicks from the lower container to the aggregate holding the seedlings in the upper container.

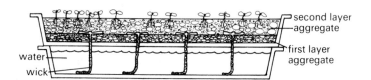

other requirements
In addition to the main items, you will need a few cheap accessories. A plastic bowl is useful for draining containers and flushing out accumulated salts now and then. Since it is only used for waste, any bowl will do. Just make sure it is big enough to hold as much solution as you intend to put into any one container.

Some sort of watering-can is necessary—the size and shape will depend on how many and how large your plants are. For indoor gardening or window boxes, a long spout is almost essential; for roof-tops or garden systems, the ordinary kind may be used, as long as it has not been contaminated with weedkiller or other chemical mixtures. A small jug will help to mix the powder thoroughly before you put it in the can.

For the rest, use whatever you would normally need for the care of house-plants—small bamboo canes for staking vines or large specimens, and soft twine or paper-covered wire twists for tying the stems up, a soft brush for pollinating some fruit plants, a small fork for holding tiny plants which are being transplanted, a notebook to keep a record of when and where and how your plant family is developing, a small spray for misting plants during very dry spells—and so on.

setting up your garden
You have chosen your container, and filled it with aggregate or solution. For your first hydroponic units, you will probably want to use plants you already have, or perhaps a new gift in its florist's wrapping. By the way, you should always quarantine a new arrival for a least a week, or preferably two. Check it carefully for any signs of pests or disease before you add it to your plant community—it is much easier to cure such problems before they spread.

The first point is to remember that you don't need soil in your new garden. Turning the pot or container upside down, ease the plant out gently, with your fingers on either side of the main stem. Now rinse the plant gently under slowly running water, not too cold. If the soil is really compacted, then let the roots soak for a while in a bowl until they seem clean. But then do it twice more so that you can be sure that not a single particle of earth is left clinging to the smallest root.

If the plant is quite small, it can be carefully inserted into the aggregate, after you have first made a hole with the handle of a knife or a small trowel; drop in the plant, and then carefully and very gently push the aggregate back until the plant is set firmly in its base.

When transferring large plants this way, it is best to make the change even slower; after cleaning the roots of all soil, let the plant rest in a bowl, and add enough plain water, without any additives, to cover the roots completely. A piece of charcoal will keep the water reasonably clear.

Let the plant rest for a few days away from your other pots. Turn up the leaves and look for the tiny webs of spider mites, or the speckling caused by sucking aphids. Only when the plant remains healthy and the roots and leaves show signs of new growth is it ready to go into its proper container. Then gradually increase the strength of the nutrient solution, starting from a quarter strength, to the full recommended dose.

It is even better to grow your own plants from seeds or cuttings, as they are acclimatized to their water garden from the very first, and are able to draw additional nourishment and strength so soon that they will fast outstrip ordinary plants brought in from outside.

To grow plants from seed, it is best to adapt fairly shallow plastic pans such as cake boxes or even new cat-litter containers which can be bought at the pet shop. First heat a skewer or metal knitting needle and push it through the plastic along the sides, about $\frac{1}{2}''$ from the bottom—these are the drainage holes. Plug the holes with plasticine or a similar substance. You will also need a tray to hold any spillage, a little larger than the container and about $1''$ deep.

Put a layer of small pebbles or large chips (or the usual clean, broken flower-pot pieces) on the bottom to prevent the finer aggregate from clogging up the holes. Now fill almost to the top with your chosen material; for sowing it is best to use small chips, gravel or vermiculite-type growing medium. Moisten carefully with plain water; a can with a rose is best as it does not disturb the surface. Let the water gradually moisten the entire box, and after about an hour pull out the drainage plugs and let the excess liquid seep out.

Now you are ready to sow. If you want a number of plants, then it is best to sow in a box such as we have just described. This is particularly true of salad crops or plants for cut flowers. Then transfer the seedlings when they are large enough. Otherwise you may sow direct into the container for ornamental plants, following the same preliminary moistening of the aggregate, and planting two seeds just in case germination is slow or difficult.

The seeds themselves should be placed on the surface, and then covered gently with a thin layer of fine, moist aggregate. They need to be protected from light. Germination is usually better than in ordinary soil, so don't sow too thickly or you will have dozens of thin, spindly plants competing for light. Larger seeds can be pushed down gently into the surface—but no more than $\frac{1}{2}''$, and then covered by raking the aggregate smooth.

Successful sowing relies at this stage on keeping the growing medium nicely moist but not too wet or dry. Of course, you will need to check your tiny plants more carefully and more often than full-grown specimens, but unless you are really careless and forget to water for a few days, the $\frac{1}{2}''$ depth below the drainage holes should hold enough liquid to keep the box just moist. Germination time will vary, depending on the type of plant, from a few days to a few weeks, or even a few months if you're ambitious enough to try some of the more difficult species. With very young plants, treat them as babies on demand feeding, and if conditions seem difficult, then change your feeding routine until they begin to grow happily again. As long as the aggregate is aerated regularly, most of the problems with soil-raised seedlings won't exist. Normally, daily feeding should be enough, dropping down to twice a week and then to once a week for sturdy well-acclimatized plants.

For regular watering once a week establish a routine for a complete change of solution for every plant. Drain off the solution by pulling out the plug, or tipping it out, depending on the container. Let the plant remain dry for an hour or so to allow the roots to breathe—this rest period aerates the growing medium, and prevents any tendency to over-wetting or rotting, especially in the summer; then replace the plug, where necessary, and put in the freshly made liquid.

At the beginning, you should check your pots every day, until you learn how quickly the solution is absorbed. The aggregate should never be allowed to dry out completely, and in general most plants prefer a lightly damp growing medium. There are individual varieties which need more or less solution, so the routine can be adapted, and of course in a hot room evaporation will be faster. But after a very short time you will learn how to adjust the amount.

Of course, if you are growing larger, food-producing plants such as tomatoes or lettuce, then the plant will absorb more nutrient, and solution should be added twice a week. In any case, after the seedlings have emerged, let the liquid drain off once a week and throw the waste away. As with the larger plants, the box should rest for an hour or two at least before you re-plug the holes and add freshly made solution.

Remember to check the name of each plant in a good gardening guide for its likes and dislikes as far as temperature and light are concerned—these don't change no matter how you grow them.

And there you are—you've provided your plants with the ideal food in the best possible conditions. A few minutes' work a week, and you should be rewarded with a leafy forest no matter where you live.

choosing your plants

Almost all plants may be adapted to hydroponic growth, but obviously some types are more suitable for your particular conditions than others. For an ordinary house-plant and flower display, here are some easily-grown examples for the beginner.

BEGONIAS are a little difficult to grow from seed, as they dislike cold and direct light almost equally. Nonetheless, once established they are a beautiful choice with an almost unending display of flowers and colour throughout the year. They make lovely pot plants, and the smaller trailing varieties are especially suitable for hanging baskets, troughs, or plant stands. The tender species used in the house are best kept away from direct sunlight, so they do particularly well in apartments.

ASTERS and CARNATIONS *(Dianthus caryophyllus)* are easy to grow in the hydroponic manner, and have been used in large-scale commercial units. Provided that temperatures stay fairly even, they will need generous amounts of nutrition, responding with perfectly formed blooms and, from the carnations, rich scents.

BULBS grow extremely well under hydroculture. As long as aeration is properly attended to none of the ordinary soil pests which are such a scourge of these plants get a chance, and the reward is bowls of fragrance and beauty all year round. Bulbs carry most of their nutrition inside their rounded shapes, so they will bloom well the first year if the water has no added nutrients. However, if you want your Hyacinths to bloom again, then proper feeding must be attended to, following the usual routine for all hydrocultured plants. Another advantage is that bulbs can be easily supported in very little aggregate. Don't stop with the common listings of Daffodils, Tulips and Hyacinths, which have been specially prepared for forcing; these can be your basic floral display, but look for special kinds, especially miniatures, which add so much fun and unexpected beauty to your garden. These include the minature Iris *(I. reticulata, I. danfordiae)*, and jonquils 'Tête à Tête', 'Baby Moon', 'April Tears', etc, Muscari, species Tulips, Freesias, whose delicate multi-coloured flowers can fill a whole house with scent, and the huge Amaryllis, with spectacular trumpets on rather coarse, ugly stems. Some of the smaller Lilies are very successful, and the difficult kinds which are so particular and curl up if a bag of lime is so much as carried into the room are much easier to grow in a hydroponic pot, as long as the aggregate is coarse enough to allow for good aeration when the water is changed.

All bulbs, because of their basic packaging of nutrition and flower bud, are good beginner's plants; they very seldom fail to flower for the first year, at least.

CACTI and other succulents are a widely known special interest of many house-plant lovers. Their strange shapes and forms are in strong contrast with most leafy, soft, green plants, and they are really best in a separate display, preferably on an aggregate of small gravel or coarse sand. This gives them a background close to their natural environment. Cacti range from tiny miniatures no more than an inch or two high to substantial 'Signposts' which given a chance will grow through your skylight to reach the sunshine. So make sure when you buy your plant that you know exactly what type it is. They are not too easy for beginners to grow from seed. Although germination is quick the young plants are extremely slow-growing and likely to dry out or rot; so stick to bought plants for a while. (Remember, as we recommended earlier, to isolate all new arrivals for a week or preferably two in quarantine.) Most Cacti are hardy and will withstand difficult conditions, and although they are usually associated with burning desert sun, some will tolerate semi-shade in an office or home, as long as the temperature doesn't fall too low (45–55°F or 7–13°C). But they will only flower if there is enough light, and as their flowers are often spectacularly beautiful, it is worth trying to find a sunny spot for your collection.

Cacti are often grown for their unusual spines and hairs, and fascinating shapes. Many of these have brilliant or attractive flowers as well. For example, *Creocereus trollii* has a lovely hairy pelt, with long red spines poking through the covering, while *Echinocactus grusonii* has long, golden-yellow spines, and grows into a largish plant. *Aporocactus flagelliformis*, sometimes called the 'rat-tail cactus', has stange, long, thin stems that straggle over the edge of the pot, but in the early spring these are covered with gleaming red flowers, and because of this it is best set high upon a shelf or in a swinging basket or planter. *Rebutia miniscula* is tiny with orange-red flowers that are almost bigger than the plant itself—unlike most Cacti, this will flower early, sometimes only two years from seed.

The Epiphyllum hybrids are a special group of cactus with spectacular Orchid-like flowers, and there are many hybrids with various-coloured flowers. The plants are very uninteresting but they make up for it with colour and scent in abundance during flowering time. A good idea is to keep these in trays small enough to move around easily, so that they can be kept in a spare room or back window when 'resting' and just brought out during their season. But remember they need a little more moisture than most Cacti, and the temperature shouldn't fall below 55°F (13°C) at any time.

One extra point. If you are going to specialize in Cacti, invest in a pair of really heavy work-gloves for your weekly routine feeding and aeration.

CITRUS FRUITS, such as dwarf lemons and oranges, are lovely shrubs for the hydroponic garden—the leaves are dark evergreen, the flowers often scented, and the tiny, unusually sour fruits can be quite pleasant in a dessert or a fruit cup.

CYCLAMEN make good pot plants since they bloom in winter—the leaves are often marbled with silver, and some species *(C. neapolitum,* for example) are beautifully scented.

FUCHSIAS have appeared in a whole slew of new hybrids during the past few years, and the range of colour and leaf-texture has widened considerably. There are many new, freely-flowering varieties with white, pink and lilac combinations, and their greatest asset is the long length of flowering season plus the profusion of delicate hanging flowers, especially good for high-level trays or display stands, where they can trail down over the sides.

IVY *(Hedera and other genera)* is one of the oldest and most underrated house plants, so why not try for some of the newer and more unusual varieties? Many have tiny deeply cut or variegated leaves, some have new leaves of golden yellow guaranteed to brighten up the most north-facing kitchen. Make sure there is always a little moisture in the air (not a bad idea for almost all your plants) by having bowls of water over the radiators or some similar kind of humidifier. Other ivies need little light, and only a moderate temperature.

NEANTHE, a dwarf palm properly known as *Collinia elegans*, is fairly hardy, and will withstand ordinary room conditions well—do not put into direct sunlight, unless only for a few hours. Keep the air moist.

GERANIUMS are properly known as 'Pelargonium'; new hybrids have given us hundreds of possibilities with a colour range from white to darkest red, including subtle tones of apricot, salmon and mixtures. Some have scented leaves (useful for candy and jelly-making). There are so many types now that geraniums chosen carefully will give you flowers all the year round.

ALUMINIUM PLANT is the common name of *Pilea cadierei*. Its silver leaves make a marvellous contrast with other green-leaved plants, and should be included in a grouping or display for best effect.

POINSETTIAS, *Euphorbia pulcherrima*, are the obvious Christmas gift, but blooming in the winter add a lovely glowing colour to our holiday tables and displays. The biggest problem is likely to be too little light, and too dry air.

ROSES have always grown well in hydroponic systems, but in the house it is probably best to keep to the dwarf varieties which only grow about 12–18″ tall. The flowers are usually like single roses and the scent is somewhat evasive, but they make charming and delicate plants, easy to care for.

Besides all these, there are the well-known house-plants, too numerous to mention, which can be found in any good book on the subject (there is a list for further reading at the back of this book). Almost every plant will adapt well to hydroponic systems—just remember that their likes and dislikes will remain the same no matter how their roots are growing.

propagation

Propagation is by any of the usual methods—cuttings, seed, grafting, layering etc. For seeds and cuttings follow the instructions in any good gardening book, remembering that you will use inert aggregate instead of compost and therefore start feeding as soon as germination takes place. You can let the seedlings develop more closer to one another than in ordinary soil. Cuttings will root quickly supported by aggregate and fed with nutrients.

Both seedlings and cuttings need more attention than large mature plants—they should be checked twice a day and more in very hot weather, and sprayed lightly with water when necessary to keep the leaves nicely damp.

larger systems for vegetable and fruit crops

Just as ordinary house-plants often grow more vigorously and develop better in a controlled hydroponic system, the same principle can easily be applied to larger gardening projects. In the past, hydroponics was a product of commercial and agricultural research and modern experience has shown that home gardeners can take advantage of it for their backyards or rooftops, as well as for house-plants and flowers.

What are the special points that make hydroponics so useful for vegetable and most fruit crops?

First, and probably most important in this inflationary world, cropping can be increased by at least 100% per square foot, with less maintenance and fewer problems. Window-boxes, rooftops, balconies, cellars, attics, all can have units which grow large and small crops.

Second, the choice of crop need not be dependent on soil type—you can grow acid-loving blueberries next to acid-hating potatoes, and both on top of rock or desert.

Third, although the initial installation may be more expensive and more complex than just digging a trench, it need not be elaborate or prohibitively expensive, and maintenance can be kept to a minimum.

Fourth, rapid growth and maturity can add an extra crop in a season with fresher texture and more flavour.

Fifth, for the environmentalist, far fewer sprays are needed since weeding is eliminated and heavy gasoline engines for mechanical tilling and ploughing are not used.

We will show you in the following page three systems suitable for a wide variety of uses: a small frame or 'mini-greenhouse' for propagation and small shallow-rooting salad greens; a tomato, melon or cucumber bed, for one side of a greenhouse or outdoors; and a larger garden plan, based on three 10′×4′ beds for a wide variety of outdoor crops.

The principles are always the same for all types of hydroponic gardens. The growing medium is a stable, inert structure, and nutrient-enriched water carries food to the plant either continually or periodically. In any case the nutrient must be renewed regularly and the aggregate should never be allowed to dry out completely or to remain waterlogged for any length of time.

small frame, mini-greenhouse or propagator

This compact system is designed for use at shelf height. It saves bending and stooping over the tiny plants and allows use of a very simple but effective gravity-feed method, which is easier than hand-watering, but must be attended to once in the morning and once in the evening.

Build an open box for the top of your staging (about 2′ 6″×4′) or put it on legs at a comfortable height. It must be 6″ deep and water-tight, so line it with zinc or heavy butyl rubber. A hole drilled in one side 2″ above the base should be large

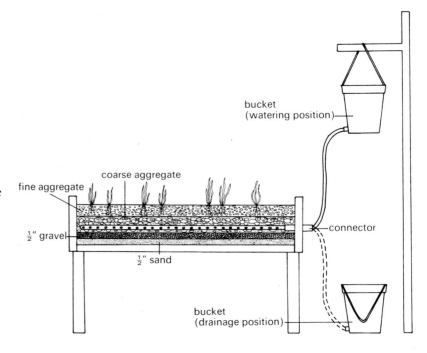

A small frame system showing the bucket for the nutrient in two positions—when it is placed in the upper position the nutrient will flow into the bed; when it is on the ground, much of the nutrient will drain back into the bucket, to allow aeration of the aggregate.

bucket
(watering position)

coarse aggregate

fine aggregate

½″ gravel

½″ sand

connector

bucket
(drainage position)

enough to take a double-ended hose-connector, glued in place with plastic resin or a waterproof compound.

Line the box with $\frac{1}{2}''$ of sand. If you are using this as a propagator, lay soil-warming cables on the sand as directed in the instructions, then cover with another $\frac{1}{2}''$ of coarser gravel. Now attach about 10' of perforated hose to the inside connector, and coil around the box to distribute the nutrient. The open end should be covered with fine mesh. Now add aggregate of a fairly coarse kind to cover the hose, topping it with 1" of finer aggregate—either peat or fine gravel.

The other end of the hose-connector is attached to a hose and to a bucket with a handle. The hose must be long enough to allow the bucket to be hooked above the unit and alternatively put on the ground. When the bucket is hooked above, the nutrient flows down again into the bucket draining the aggregate and letting it aerate.

It is best to let the solution flood the tank in the morning, then lower the bucket and let it drain from late afternoon. The solution may have to be topped up in warm weather, or if the aggregate is very retentive. Experiment with clear water at first before you add any seeds or plants to see how much solution will dampen all the aggregate without making it soggy or too wet. Then keep the liquid up to that amount, changing to fresh solution every week.

tomato bed

This is an automated version of the previous system which is very useful and extremely easy to operate. A planter box is built up on the ground for a small bed, about 8" deep. Again, make it fit your convenience, either as a greenhouse border or in the open, but keep the width 3' or less, and the length about 2-3" from one end to the other.

At the lower end, drill a drainage hole for a hose or pipe outlet, protected from gravel with a fine mesh cap. This should be about one inch from the base. Line the box as before with plastic, zinc or butyl rubber, then put in a 2" layer of coarse aggregate, pebbles or small shards of broken pottery (cleaned and sterilized!). Top with your chosen growing aggregate.

Now a large tank or reservoir must be positioned next to the lower end; if you don't want to bother with a return valve, dig a hole and let the tank about 36" into the ground, so that the drainage pipe attached to the drainage hole is above the level of solution in the reservoir. (A new plastic dustbin is a good reservoir, complete with cover to keep the solution clear.) A small pump (the type used for underwater fountains and waterfalls) is dropped into the reservoir, attached to a long pipe which runs out of the tank along the side of the bed and then is turned back to flow out at the top of the bed. A timer on the pump will operate at set times, two or three times a day, to flood the bed. Then it turns itself off and the water gradually runs back into the reservoir until the next flooding.

Try out the system before you add the plants, checking to see how long the pump must run to flood the bed and how often the bed must be flooded to keep it moist but not sopping wet during most of the day. If the unit is outdoors, a hot summer may require more flooding, and heavy rainfall may dilute the solution so that it needs renewing. Sensitive 'leaf' cells are available which register dryness on the surface, and which can be rigged to trigger the pump. But especially in a protected environment the basic system is simple and efficient.

Heavy rain outdoors may upset the water-nutrient balance. So unprotected gardens are built with extra drainage holes all round to help water drain quickly; nutrients might have to be mixed and added more often. A siphon nozzle attached to a tap and a reservoir of highly concentrated liquid nutrient is a good idea for large-scale watering. All sorts of automated gadgets can be fitted to turn the tap on and off, check the dilution level of the nutrient and the rate of flow etc.

Hydroponics can lead you from a simple pot plant to a complex continuous flow unit 100' long. It has advantages for everyone, as a way to keep Aunt Agatha's rubber plant happy, an easy-maintenance, no-fuss, no-mess means of growing a window-full of plants or a bumper crop of vegetables, herbs and flowers at minimum cost and effort, or as a scientific hobby with experiments, new methods, notes and records for 'hydro-bugs' everywhere.

useful plant groupings

These lists of plants mentioned in the book are not exhaustive, but will provide a useful general guide when you are planning visual effects. For further details of individual plants look up the page references given for each name in the Index.

floating

Aldrovandia vesiculosa (also submersive)
Azolla caroliniana
Ceratopteris thalictroides (also emersive)
Eichhornia crassipes
Hydrocharis Morsus-ranae
Lemna minor
Limnobium spongia
Pistia stratiotes
Riccia fluitans
Salvinia auriculata
Stratiotes aloides
Trapa natans
Utricularia exoleta
Utricularia vulgaris
Vesicularia dubyana

mainly submersive

Acorus calamus (marginal in nature, submersive in aquarium)
Acorus gramineus (marginal in nature, submersive in aquarium)
Aldrovandia vesiculosa
Ceratophyllum demersum
Cryptocoryne nevilii (emersive outdoors)
Echinodorus berteroi (emersive or trailing outdoors)
Echinodorus brevipedicellatus (emersive outdoors)
Eleocharis acicularis
Fontinalis antipyretica
Isoetes lacustris
Najas minor
Nitella flexilis
Potamogeton crispus
Potamogeton filiformis
Potamogeton lucens
Sagittaria subulata forma portugalensis
Vallisneria spiralis

mainly emersive

Alisma plantago
Anubias congensis
Anubias lanceolata
Aponogeton bernieranus
Aponogeton crispus
Aponogeton elongatus
Aponogeton fenestralis
Aponogeton ulvaceus
Aponogeton undulatus
Bacopa monniera
Ceratopteris thalictroides (can also float)
Crassula aquatica
Cryptocoryne balansae
Cryptocoryne beckettii
Cryptocoryne blassii
Cryptocoryne ciliata
Cryptocoryne cordata
Cryptocoryne grandis
Cryptocoryne johorensis
Cryptocoryne nevilii (submersive indoors)
Cryptocoryne undulata
Cryptocoryne willisii
Echinodorus cordifolius
Echinodorus longistylus
Echinodorus martii
Hippuris vulgaris
Hottonia palustris
Hydrocotyle vulgaris
Lagenandra ovata
Lobelia dortmanna
Lycopodium inundatum
Marsilea hirsuta
Marsilea quadrifolia
Orontium aquaticum
Sagittaria guyanensis
Sagittaria latifolis
Subularia aquatica
Vesicularia dubyana

trailing (flower and/or leaves can float on water surface)

Ambulia heterophylla
Brasenia schreberi
Cabomba aquatica
Cardamina lyrata
Ceratophyllum demersum
Elisma natans
Elodea canadensis
Heterantha dubia
Hydrocleis nymphaeoides
Isoetes malinvernia
Ludwigia palustris
Myriophyllum elatinoides
Myriophyllum spicatum
Myriophyllum verticillatum
Nuphar luteum
Nuphar pumillum
Nymphaea alba
Nymphaeoides aquatica
Ottelia alismoides
Ruppia maritima

marginal plants

Acorus calamus (can be submerged in aquarium)
Acorus gramineus (can be submerged in aquarium)
Alisma plantago
Bacopa amplexicaulis (emersive in aquarium)
Bacopa monniera (emersive in aquarium)
Calla palustris
Eleocharis acicularis (can be submerged in aquarium)
Ludwigia natans (also emersive in aquarium)
Ludwigia palustris (trailing in aquarium)
Rorippa amphibia
Sagittaria latifolia
Sagittaria montividensis
Sagittaria sagittifolia
Saururus cernuus
Sparganium americanum
Sparganium erectum

suppliers

Here is a small selection of stockists of fish-tank supplies and aquatic plants. If there is none listed below in your area, many of those given will be happy to mail plants to you, or advise you of wholesale or retail stockists in your locality.

Great Britain

Fish Tanks Ltd, 49 Blandford St, London W1H 3AF (01-935 9432)
Walter R. Smith, 39 Tib St, Manchester M4 1LX
The Goldfish Bowl, 118 Magdalen Rd, Oxford
Shirley Aquatics Ltd, Stratford Rd, Monkspath, Shirley, West Midlands
J.M.C. Aquatics, 59 Stubley Lane, Dronfield, Sheffield
Hemmingways Pet Shop Ltd, 56 Wellington Road, Dewsbury, Yorkshire
Betta Aquaria, 108 Shields Rd, Newcastle-upon-Tyne
London Aquatic Co. Ltd, Greenwood Nurseries, Theobalds Park Road, Enfield, Middlesex (wholesalers)
R. J. Cook Ltd, Shaw St, Hill Top, West Bromwich, Staffs. (wholesalers)
C. Murray, 95 Commerce St, Glasgow 5, Scotland (wholesalers)

United States

Crystal Aquarium, 1438 3rd Avenue, New York, NY
Fish Town USA, 145 Nassau St, New York, NY; Flushing, Long Island; Ramsey, NJ.
Aquarium Stock Co, 31 Warren St, New York, NY
Ed's Tropical Aquariums, Forest Hills, NY; Livingston, NJ; Yonkers, NY.
Three Springs Fisheries, Lilypond, Md
Hermitage Gardens, Canastota, NY
Paradise Gardens, Whitman, Maine
Slocum Water Gardens, Winter Haven, Fla.
William Tricker, Saddle River, NJ
Van Ness Water Gardens, Uplands, Ca.

books to read

Beginner's Guide to Hydroponics, by J. S. Douglas (Pelham, London, 1972)
Encyclopedia of Water Plants, by Dr J. Stodola (TFH Publications, Neptune City, NJ, 1967)
Gardening Indoors Under Lights, by F. H. and J. L. Kranz (Viking, New York, 1971)
Garden Perennials and Water Plants, by A. J. Huxley (Blandford, London, 1971)
Garden Pools, Fountains and Waterfalls (Lane, Menloe Pk, Calif., 1974)
Hydroponics: Gardening Without Soil, by D. Harris (Purnell, New York, 1969)
Magic of Hydroponics for the Home Gardener, by Bridewell (Woodbridge, Loma Linda, Calif. 1972)
Modern Water Gardening, by R. Kaye (Faber, London, 1973)
Pond Life in the Aquarium, by H. Janus (Van Nostrand Reinhold, New York, 1966)
Water Gardening, by J. Kramer (Scribner, New York, 1971)
Water in the Garden, by D. Bartrum (Branford, Newton Center, MA, and Gifford, London, 1968)
Water Lilies, Goldfish Pools and Tropical Fishes, by G. L. Thomas (TFH Publications, Neptune City, NJ, 1965)

picture acknowledgements

Permission to reproduce photographs has kindly been given by the following (the page numbers in italics refer to colour illustrations).

Heather Angel: 82, *90, 94* (both). Siegfried Böker: 32. Bruce Coleman Ltd: Bruce Coleman 86; Jennifer Fry 80. By kind permission of The House of Rochford: 113 (both). Harry Smith Horticultural Photographic Collection: 98.

The following photographs were specially taken for the book by Alwyn Bailey: 104, 106. A. C. Cooper Ltd, London: 21 (both), 22, 24 (all), 25, *34, 38, 42, 46, 50, 54-5, 58, 62, 66, 70, 75, 78-9.*

index